The Digital Classroom

The way students learn changes when they have access to digital tools. *The Digital Classroom* demonstrates that using technology to enhance students' learning is not dependent on a specific learning management system or software – it is about changing the pedagogy with the help of an arsenal of useful tools and methods.

This practical book introduces easy to use methods to all teachers in digital classrooms with the intention to make it simple, accessible, and achievable for everyone. It is not only about the tools, and the how and why, but also about changing the pedagogy making the learning more relevant to the students. When you open the classroom to the rest of the world, the teacher becomes more important than ever. Topics in the book include:

- Technology and deeper learning
- Social media in the global classroom
- Building a personal learning network
- The flipped classroom and cooperative learning
- The use of iPads in primary and middle school
- Teaching with videogames
- Special education
- Digital citizenship

Digital tools can play a key role in making learning happen and what the teachers know about the use of technology is key. *The Digital Classroom* will be of great interest to teachers and trainee teachers who wish to develop their digital competency by using the book as part of their professional learning.

Ann S. Michaelsen is a school administrator at Sandvika High School in Oslo. She has more than 25 years of experience of teaching with technology and was a school leader from 2006, starting a school that pioneered having 1:1 laptops for 900 students. Ann is currently also working part time with the University of Oslo, Department for Research, Innovation and Competence Development.

Ann Michaelsen's insightful book gives a terrific overview about how education is being transformed in the new, post-pandemic era. This book will give you great ideas for both classroom and administrator perspectives on improving outreach to students online.
– **Barbara Ann Oakley**, Professor of Engineering, Oakland University, USA

Teachers will never be replaced by technology. But after COVID-19, teachers who don't use some technology will be replaced by ones who do. Thoughtful, practical, and magnificently sensible, this is a book that educators will not want to put down once they start it.
– **Andy Hargreaves**, Visiting Professor, University of Ottawa, Canada

The best part about this book is that the author has put in her own experiences on how she herself has used technology as an effective tool for teaching and learning. It is a helpful guide for those who want to use it more effectively as educators or as learners.
– **Shakeel Ahmad**, Co-Founder Mind Mingle, India

This book is a vital addition to an educator's professional library. The focus on both tools and pedagogy provides an essential bridge into teaching and learning modes that are digital, online, and networked. There are no excuses left, and nowhere to hide, every teacher must upskill and become confident in digital-first learning, and this book leads the way in supporting that requirement.
– **Julie Lindsay**, Associate Director, Digital Learning Innovation, University of Southern Queensland, Australia

The global pandemic has hit education like an earthquake, with aftershocks continuing to rattle expectations of what school should be. By sharing lessons learned, this book from Ann Michaelsen will help us seize the opportunity for lasting transformation of teaching and learning.
– **Suzie Boss**, Author of *Reinventing Project-Based Learning*, 3rd edition

The Digital Classroom
Transforming the Way We Learn

Ann S. Michaelsen

LONDON AND NEW YORK

First published 2021
by Routledge
2 Park Square, Milton Park, Abingdon, Oxon OX14 4RN

and by Routledge
52 Vanderbilt Avenue, New York, NY 10017

Routledge is an imprint of the Taylor & Francis Group, an informa business

© 2021 Ann S. Michaelsen

The right of Ann S. Michaelsen to be identified as author of this work has been asserted by her in accordance with sections 77 and 78 of the Copyright, Designs and Patents Act 1988.

All rights reserved. No part of this book may be reprinted or reproduced or utilised in any form or by any electronic, mechanical, or other means, now known or hereafter invented, including photocopying and recording, or in any information storage or retrieval system, without permission in writing from the publishers.

Trademark notice: Product or corporate names may be trademarks or registered trademarks, and are used only for identification and explanation without intent to infringe.

British Library Cataloguing-in-Publication Data
A catalogue record for this book is available from the British Library

Library of Congress Cataloging-in-Publication Data
Names: Michaelsen, Ann S., author.
Title: The digital classroom : transforming the way we learn / Ann S. Michaelsen.
Description: Abingdon, Oxon ; New York, NY : Routledge, [2021] | Includes bibliographical references and index.
Identifiers: LCCN 2020038808 | ISBN 9780367611057 (hardback) | ISBN 9780367611071 (paperback) | ISBN 9781003104148 (ebook)
Subjects: LCSH: Mobile communication systems in education. | Education--Effect of technological innovations on.
Classification: LCC LB1044.84 .M55 2021 | DDC 371.33--dc23
LC record available at https://lccn.loc.gov/2020038808

ISBN: 978-0-367-61105-7 (hbk)
ISBN: 978-0-367-61107-1 (pbk)
ISBN: 978-1-003-10414-8 (ebk)

Typeset in Bembo
by SPi Gloal, India

Contents

Acknowledgments   *vii*
Contributors   *ix*

    Introduction: A significant change in teaching and learning   1
    Ann S. Michaelsen

1   Learning in the digital classroom   4
    Ann S. Michaelsen

2   Digital tools for the classroom   16
    Ann S. Michaelsen

3   Social media in the global classroom   37
    Ann S. Michaelsen

4   Tablet PCs in primary and middle school   51
    Simen Spurkland

5   Cooperative learning   60
    Ann S. Michaelsen

6   The flipped classroom   69
    Ann S. Michaelsen

7   Teaching with video games   78
    Aleksander Husøy and Tobias Staaby

8	Digital citizenship *Ann S. Michaelsen*	88
9	Special needs education *Ann S. Michaelsen*	101
10	The digital classroom: what is the insight from contemporary educational research? *Marte Blikstad-Balas*	110
Index		121

Acknowledgments

This book highlights the importance of personal learning networks and the power of connections. The same applies to the writing of this book. *The Digital Classroom: Transforming the Way We Learn* would never have been written or published if I had not met so many amazing people during my 25 years in education. A special thanks to Moliehi Sekese in Lesotho; our friendship has resulted in life-altering changes for students in Lesotho and Norway, represented by a former student at Sandvika High School, Tobias Langås Handeland, in this book. And a great thank you to our student Elise Groth who contributed to the choice of book cover with her expertise in design. The talents of our students never cease to amaze me.

Thanks to the four co-writers who all have added valuable insight into essential parts of the digital classroom. And thanks to the teachers who wrote shorter texts with practical classroom examples. Thanks to Troy Hicks, who introduced me to his publisher in the United States; she guided me in the right direction that eventually led to the publication of this book. Thanks to all the dedicated educators around the world that I have met; your relentless devotion to your students is inspiring. Investing in the future is the only solution to solving the problems our generation has left behind.

This book is dedicated to the next generation represented by my two grandchildren, Julia Kallåk Michaelsen and Wilhelm Alexander Michaelsen Dupuy. I hope that your years in school will inspire you and provide the confidence and skills needed to solve the challenges of the future and where learning will be both fun and rewarding at the same time.

Contributors

Aleksander Husøy is a teacher of English and Social Science at Nordahl Grieg Upper Secondary School in Bergen, Norway. Husøy has made extensive use of games in his own classroom for the past 10 years and is a leading voice in the field of games in education. Husøy also works as a specialist instructor in game pedagogy for Vestland County.

Marte Blikstad-Balas is a professor (full) at in the The Department of Education, University of Oslo, Norway. Her key research interests revolve around literacy in school -— and hos how digitalizations changes teaching. She has published over more than 30 scientific articles. Her latest publication is.. Blikstad-Balas, M., & Klette, K. (2019). Still a long way to go. Nordic Journal of Digital Literacy, 15(01), 55–68.

Simen Spurkland is a teacher at Hennummarka lower secondary school i Lier, Norway. Through his 20 years of teaching, Simen has taught a wide range of subjects from maths to music, social studies to English as second language and P.E to Home Ec. Since 2013, Simen has been teaching in classes with 1:1 iPads. The last years, Simen has been giving lectures, courses and keynotes on how to implement digital devices in the classroom and shared his experiences with what significant changes that can be made when a device is used right.

Tobias Staaby is a PhD candidate at the University of Bergen, Norway, where he is writing a dissertation on video games in education. Prior to starting his PhD education, he worked as a high school teacher, teaching Norwegian language and literature, religious studies, and history. Staaby has been working with games and learning for several years, giving talks and lectures and holding seminars and workshops.

Introduction

A significant change in teaching and learning

Ann S. Michaelsen

The coronavirus epidemic in 2020 became a game changer in education throughout the whole world. As of March 6, 2020, 300 million kids were impacted, according to UNESCO. By March 27, the number was 1.4 billion (UNESCO, 2020). Norway went into lockdown on March 13, and homeschooling via digital tools became the norm. For some countries, that meant little or no school at all. In Norway, almost every student had access to computers with good bandwidth, and that made it easy for teachers to teach their students. Even so, there were many obstacles, and students with difficult home conditions, many siblings, and students with learning disabilities were suffering. We do not know the long-term effects of those 2 months, and in many countries the homeschooling period was much longer.

When I first wrote this book, many teachers were still hesitant about using technology in class. The complete lockdown of schools left them with few options (see Figure 0.1). From one day to the other, everything changed. Teachers had to transform their way of teaching drastically, from traditional classroom pedagogy to an online classroom using Teams or Zoom. There soon was an abundance of software offered free for educators, and designing online classes became the new norm: Many teachers quickly got the hang of it, at least in my school. Having mastered the form and content, we slowly turned our attention toward assessment. How to assess students' work when everything was online and answers to questions were easy to Google? That became the essential question. Because this transformation was not easy, to succeed, teachers had to change their mindset when figuring out how to teach in this environment. Copying from a textbook with facts and questions was never a good idea. To help teachers, examples of how to make creative educational tasks popped up in social media and newspapers everywhere.

What we are talking about here is changing the pedagogy to suit the purpose. And that turned out to be the greatest obstacle for most teachers during the lockdown.

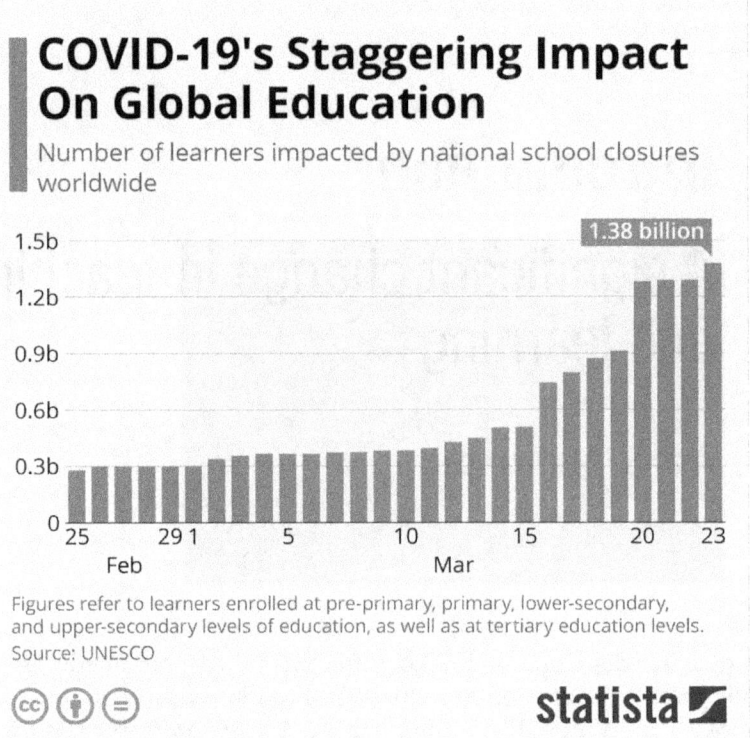

FIGURE 0.1 Number of learners impacted by national school closures worldwide.
Source: Statista

Around the world, these transformational changes were noticed, and many saw this as an opportunity for real, sustainable change.

"It's a great moment" for learning, says Andreas Schleicher, head of education at the Organisation for Economic Co-operation and Development (OECD; as quoted in Anderson, 2020). "All the red tape that keeps things away is gone, and people are looking for solutions that in the past they did not want to see," he says. Students will take ownership of their learning, understanding more about how they learn, what they like, and what support they need. They will personalize their learning, even if the systems around them won't. Schleicher believes that the genie cannot be put back in the bottle: "Real change takes place in deep crisis," he says. "You will not stop the momentum that will build" (as quoted in Anderson, 2020).

It remains to see if the head of education at OECD is right. I think these months in 2020 have given us an exceptional opportunity to change schools, but I am not so sure that this is a priority in many countries right now. What I do know is that many teachers around the world have improved their digital skills. And I know teachers were looking forward to returning to school and continuing to use digital tools for learning. The months of homeschooling have truly become a game changer. Many teachers are better equipped to use technology in their classrooms. These months of trial and error might very well have provided much of the training teachers needed.

Marte Blikstad-Balas addresses this in Chapter 10; most teachers do not feel that their professor teacher education has prepared them to use digital technology in their classrooms:

Now is the time to use this momentum to make a difference, and I would like to quote Andreas Schleicher "Now is the time to "to help students take ownership of their learning" (as quoted in Anderson, 2020) because that is the clue. It is all about giving students voice and choice. I think we are ready for that to happen now. This book will hopefully supplement teachers' need for professional development and provide an additional toolbox for teachers now familiar with the digital classroom.

References

Anderson, J. (2020, March 30). *The coronavirus pandemic is reshaping education.* From QUARTZ: https://qz.com/1826369/how-coronavirus-is-changing-education/

UNESCO. (2020, June 7). *Education: From disruption to recovery.* From UNESCO Building Peace in the Minds of Men and Women: https://en.unesco.org/covid19/educationresponse

CHAPTER 1

Learning in the digital classroom

Ann S. Michaelsen

Introduction

This book will show you how to use digital tools to enhance student learning. My background is both as an English teacher, a school leader at Sandvika High School in Oslo, Norway, author and speaker. I have many years of experience teaching in a digital classroom. Our school was new in 2006, and the year after, we became a 1:1 bring-your-own-device school. Everyone has a computer, and the ratio now is about 50–50 Mac versus PC. At the same time, we introduced block scheduling, meaning that we teach mostly one and no more than two subjects each day. I talk about the advantages of this later on in the book. Although I teach in a high school, what I write about here applies just as much to primary and middle school because the tools and methods used here can be applied across age groups and subjects.

With this book, I want to share good examples of the use of technology in teaching. The key is to get the technology, pedagogy, and content to connect. I hope that this book can help you utilize the educational potentials of digital technology and that by reading this book, it will be easier for you to get started.

In this first chapter, I look at the use of technology in the classroom, deeper learning, students' ownership of their learning, and the global classroom. Chapters 2 and 3 show step by step how to make use of a selection of digital tools. The goal is to change what is taking place in the classroom and make learning both relevant and exciting for the students. I have concentrated on what is free or what schools most likely already have invested in. There might be a difference in what is provided for you, depending on your country. In Chapter 4, I have invited a middle school teacher to write about his experiences using iPads in class with many helpful suggestions for suitable apps. Chapters 5 and 6 take a closer look at using technology in cooperative learning and the flipped classroom, and in Chapter 7, two experts in gaming write about using computer games to learn. In Chapter 8, I show examples of how students should behave online, and I share advice on safe and practical web searches for both teachers and students. In Chapter 9, I take a closer look at pedagogy and technology designed to make learning with computers more accessible and how technology can help our more vulnerable students. Chapter 10 offers insight from a professor at the University of Oslo on how research ties into the way I work with my students in the classroom.

Technology in school

Using technology has become a natural part of our everyday life, but technology requires new ways of teaching and teachers who know how to adapt. Classroom management is more critical to succeeding now that every student has access to a device. One solution could be to control students' use of technology in school by limiting access to the internet. Many would probably agree that this is not the best solution. Try searching for private networks at your school, and you will see that students have access to private Wi-Fi everywhere. A mobile phone in your pocket can easily be used to create private networks. Many schools have resorted to what they call mobile phone hotels. At our school, we have these mobile phone hotels on the walls in every classroom, and students now know that they have to put their phones there when they enter the classroom. This has turned out to be a good solution, mostly because if they need phones for activities in the classroom, they are allowed to use them. We know that students can be stressed by constant messages from Facebook, Snapchat, and Instagram. And at the same time, even if we eliminate the use of mobile phones, students still have access to most of the mentioned social media on their computers. In other words, we need to be aware of how students use technology when we set up our lessons and plan accordingly.

Since I started using technology in my class in 2006, I have changed my mind about how much we should limit the online opportunities for our students. As I now see it, some students will be able to work well with full internet access, and others will not. Also, the problem with limiting internet access is that our students are entering a world filled with temptations and, later, a work environment where they need to master new digital technologies. As teachers, we can help them develop a healthy approach to sensible use in a technology-rich environment. If we are aspiring towards student-centered learning, we need to know that they can focus on learning when they are online. At our school, we experience a change in attitude among our students from the beginning of high school until graduation. The younger the students, the more you have to work with them. Self-control and knowing how you learn with technology is a process. That said, it is essential to point out that what goes on in the classroom is the teacher's responsibility. If you choose to lecture with a PowerPoint presentation, control your PC with a clicker as you move around in the classroom. Often, a glance at students who are engaging in something else is all that is needed. Should students take notes when listening to the teacher? Do they need to? Many students are good at taking notes; others are easily distracted. This can be clarified by the teacher if you ask to see the students' notes before they leave class. Students who engage in other activities on their PCs often dim the screen so that their teacher does not see what is going on. Others flip through different setups when the teacher passes by (ALT+TAB). If you are not sure what your students are doing when you are teaching, invite other teachers or administrators into your classroom to observe. This is often the basis for useful discussions, both with the observer and with students.

What goes on in the classroom – using technology – must always be planned and administrated by the teacher, preferably in close dialogue with the students. How are we using technology, when, and why? How is it helping us learn? Those are useful questions.

In my experience, to address these issues, the teacher needs a certain amount of digital competency, and many find it too challenging to keep up in this area. We all know that teachers have many tasks. Teaching is a 24/7 job, and learning new skills can seem daunting. This is where this book is meant to help. The goal is to show that digital tools can free up time and that it is possible to take small steps to get there.

A pedagogy for deeper learning

Deeper learning is a buzzword in education, at least in Norway. Deeper learning is often associated with 21-century teaching and learning. It ties well in with the methods I describe in this book. The use of technology that I address in this book is related to the new curricula for schools in Norway, implemented in 2020. The goal in Norway now is that all students should attend a school where they are able to master every subject and where what they learn is both relevant and forward-thinking and based on the concept of deeper learning. I am convinced that this is the way to approach the future of schools everywhere.

> Deeper learning is a critical and higher-order thinking model that is made up of the following six competencies: master core academic content, think critically and solve complex problems, communicate effectively, work collaboratively, learn how to learn, develop academic mindsets. Deeper learning is a manifestation of the backlash from standardized testing critics. It was developed to help students develop skill sets that would enable them to learn from, thrive, and adapt in real-world environments. Many would say that deeper learning simply describes what exemplary teachers have been doing since the beginning of time.
>
> (Lynch, 2019)

All around us, we see changes in the use of technology. We know our students will use technology when they start in their new professions. As Marte professor Blikstad-Balas states in Chapter 10,

> [t]here is general consensus that students will need to have extensive digital competence to meet the demands of any future job. There is a general agreement about the rather obvious fact that digital technology is everywhere in the Western world and that students are used to having access to such technologies in every aspect of their lives.

And we all agree that they will need to continually learn new technology, acquire new knowledge, and meet new challenges throughout their lives. We need young people who can reflect, who are critical, explorative, and creative. The challenges of the future can only be solved by people who have excellent collaboration skills and can solve complex issues. This adds up to the common understanding that deeper learning is essential in schools today.

Deeper learning means that students gradually develop their understanding of concepts and contexts within a course and across subjects. Learning processes that promote deeper learning are characterized by the fact that students can immerse themselves and work with the curriculum over time and receive feedback and challenges in line with their progress. It is also important that students reflect on their learning and can understand contexts.

(Norway, Department of Education, 2016).

Education has to be global, and the differences between countries should be marginal—the ability to work and collaborate across borders matters more now than ever.

Deeper learning means students can develop competencies that enable them to understand how different subjects relate to each other. Our goal is that students can reflect on what they have learned and build on that. We want them to connect knowledge between different sources and subjects, interpret data, think critically, and use subject-specific methods to solve problems in digital environments. Today, we all have access to an unimaginable amount of information. Integrating information elements from different sources requires cognition and understanding on a higher level. Selecting reliable information and creating coherence are, therefore, crucial skills in today's society. The next step is applying this knowledge and using it on a global scale.

There are different interpretations of the concept of deeper learning. In this book, I build on the Canadian school researcher Michael Fullan and Langworthy's (2014) interpretation of the term. He emphasizes that students must acquire a vast knowledge of the world, know how to communicate with others, and be creative. The subtitle of the book is quite clarifying: "Engage the World, Change the World." Fullan builds his concept on a handful of "global competencies" that he calls "The 6 Cs of Education": character, citizenship, collaboration, communication, creativity, and critical thinking. These general skills are also referred to as "21st-century skills."

Deep learning requires that teachers and students can look outside the classroom. To accomplish this, we have to change what goes on in the classroom. According to Fullan, we do not have a choice. He believes students will seek other alternatives if school appears irrelevant and alienating. "Increasingly, students will not tolerate boring or alienating schooling. And the dynamics of a digitized global world need radical changes, whether we like it or not," says Fullan and Langworthy (2014).

I believe that we need teachers who embrace equity, innovation, empowerment, collaboration, and risk-taking, and only then can we change the capacity of education to create a democratic, interrelated global community.

Classroom application

An example of deeper learning is how my class worked with one of the United Nations Sustainable Development Goals, Goal 13: Climate action, last year:

There is no country that is not experiencing the drastic effects of climate change. Greenhouse gas emissions are more than 50 percent higher than in 1990. Global warming is causing long-lasting changes to our climate system, which threatens irreversible consequences if we do not act.

(United Nations, 2019)

First, we wrote about how we are experiencing a change in climate in Norway, and then students translated a presentation they found on a Norwegian website into English. Then we Skyped with students in India and Israel and discussed how they were experiencing climate change in their countries. They shared their concerns with us, and my students wrote about this on their blogs. The following week we received additional comments from students in Australia on a Padlet I had shared with them, and they wrote about the drought they were experiencing in Australia at that time. We continued to explore the protests among young people in Europe that started with Greta Thunberg's appeal in Davos. I have shared this lesson plan on my blog, and my students have reflected on this way of learning on their blogs. It is easier to understand the problems in other parts of the world if we take the time to discuss with people living there. Looking back at the definition of deeper learning, we see that this lesson plan covered many of the requirements: communication, critical thinking, cooperation, innovation, and creativity.

To work like this, technology is vital, but we need to use it wisely. Technology alone will not guarantee a school for the future or prevent students from being left behind in a changing world. A digital paradigm shift constitutes a change from one way of thinking to another. When implemented correctly, digital tools can transform education.

The point is to use technology so that students develop the knowledge they need for them to become engaged and active citizens. The reason we still have many examples of technology that have not led to increased learning is that we have rarely had a plan for its use beyond accessing it. We need a new pedagogy for deeper learning, and if we are to succeed, teachers need to change what they do in the classroom. We have to create a culture that encourages learning for leaders, teachers, and students.

So I argue in this book that we need to change the pedagogy to take advantage of technology to improve learning. If the teacher continues to teach using old textbooks that have standard questions for the students to answer, then we are not moving in the right direction. If what we do in the classroom is rote memorization of facts tested in a digital multiple-choice quiz, we have not achieved much. It is so important to encourage the students to ask the questions, not the teachers.

> The research on brain activity by Rosalind Picard and her colleagues at [Massachusetts Institute of Technology]'s Media Lab suggests that students' brain activity is nearly non-existent during lectures – even lower than when they are asleep. Lectures equal brain "flatlining," and, as Professor Eric Mazur of Harvard University's Physics Department puts it, students "are more asleep during lectures than when they are in bed!" For these reasons, we need a new pedagogy.
>
> (Fullan & Langworthy, 2014)

I have examples of inviting experts into my classroom and how the quality of the conversations depended on how well the students were able to ask interesting questions.

To do so requires extensive research and knowing where to find relevant information. The best reward is when the person invited expresses that.

> What students do in the classroom is what they learn (as Dewey would say) Now, what is it that students do in the classroom? Well, mostly, they sit and listen to the teacher. Mostly, they are required to remember. It is practically unheard of for students to play any role in determining what problems are worth studying or what procedures of inquiry ought to be used. Here is the point: Once you have learned how to ask questions – relevant and appropriate and substantial questions – you have learned how to learn, and no one can keep you from learning whatever you want or need to know.
>
> (Weingartner, 1969)

The question here is, How much has this changed since 1969?

If we let students work with independent tasks that give them the role of a researcher, where they decide on what to search for and the content, and we provide the opportunity to collaborate with others, then digital technology will offer a whole new opportunity to learn.

Outside school, we see a lot of examples of this way of communicating and learning. Learning takes place in interaction with others, and digital tools play an essential role in communication and information searches. Many schools are digital, no doubt about it, but their use is often still conservative. How often are students able to be creative in their use of technology in your school? Does your school fully take advantage of how technology opens up for collaboration across schools and borders? When discussing what skills the new generation needs, creativity and innovation are often mentioned together with the use of technology. Still, it is not enough to *say* this. How do we do this? That is the challenge.

Block scheduling

My school is what we call a new school. Built and established in 2006, we aimed for an up-to-date and innovative school with extensive use of technology. Already in 2007, we started with bring-your-own-device, and it was also the year we started block scheduling. We wanted to give the students ample time to work on projects and to get into subject matters more than in traditional schools. You could say we were early adopters of deeper learning. One of our motives for doing this was also to allow time for our students to work on their computers. Everyone knows that in short timeslots like 45 minutes, there is hardly time to power up the computer to start working before the students have to go to the next class. In our school, block scheduling is usually no more than two blocks, with two subjects, each day. As an example, my English class this year is on Mondays from 08:30 until 13:10 with a half-hour lunch break from 11:00 till 11:30. Our school has done this successfully for over 12 years now, and both students and teachers love this way of working. I can drop in on any class when we have visitors and ask the students if they would recommend block scheduling. They always do, and the longer they have been students in our school (high school in Norway is 3 years), the more they like it. Since we started working like this, I have read a lot of research on how this affects students' learning.

> Learning in America is a prisoner of time. For the past 150 years, American public schools have **held time constant and let learning vary.** The rule, only rarely voiced, is simple: learn what you can in the time we make available. It should surprise no one that some bright, hard-working students do reasonably well. Everyone else – from the typical student to the dropout – runs into trouble. Time is learning's warden.
>
> (Canady & Rettig, 1996)

"How has block scheduling affected perceptions of school climate, academics/instruction, and time/materials management for students, teachers, administrators, and guidance personnel?" (McCoy, 1998). Interviews were conducted at the school with students, teachers, and administrative/counseling personnel. Results revealed several themes: block scheduling helped students feel more empowered about learning, and teachers reported more empowerment in their instructional role. More assigned homework was being completed, and teachers indicated satisfaction with the demands on their time. Findings indicate that block scheduling basically benefited all students equally, regardless of ability level (McCoy, 1998).

One of the success criteria in block scheduling is that the teacher moves from a traditional teacher-lecture classroom to more student-centered learning.

"Teachers participating in a 4 × 4 block schedule see fewer students per day, teach fewer classes per day, and have longer planning periods. Thus, teachers develop closer relationships with their students and are able to provide students with more individualized instruction" (Canady & Rettig, 1996). "Teachers waste less time on administrative tasks, such as taking roll, announcements, start-up activities, and wrap up" (Baker, 2006). "In addition to utilizing more engaging instructional strategies, teachers have time to implement more varied and authentic assessment strategies" (Baker, 2006)

As a school leader and teacher, I have to say that all of this resonates with me and our experiences at our school. Once you have started this, you will never want to go back. Not to mention that most of our teachers have at least one day without teaching, a day they can use to prepare lessons and to assess student work. In fact, our school is quite okay with our teachers working from home on some of these days.

Classroom application

This is how I can set up a lesson in English when I have the class from 08:30 to 13:10.

Writing for a real audience, about issues that matter

When students write for an authentic audience about issues that matter to them, by extension they suddenly care about sophisticated rhetorical moves, carefully selecting their words, and crafting strong rebuttals (Pandolpho, 2019).

Lesson plan
Deciding on a topic

1. Choose an issue that not only matters to you but also makes you engaged and motivated to write.

2. **Finding and Narrowing Topics**

   Try to brainstorm by answering these questions. Copy them from here and write down your answers.

   1. What made you mad in the last year?
   2. What issues are you struggling with?
   3. What are you passionate about?

3. **Starting to Write**

   1. Start out with a very clear idea in your own mind about the point you want to make.
   2. Don't choose a topic, choose an argument.

4. **Write on Your Blog**

   1. When your work is published share online.

If you need ideas, you might find some from the latest news. https://edition.cnn.com/specials/5-things

Student ownership of learning

In my classroom, I have been working extensively to draw attention to the students learning. We use the curriculum goals to plan our activities. This is how we facilitate deeper learning, as students actively participate in their learning processes. We can change what we do in the classroom, based on current events and news as long as we cover one or more of the curriculum goals. Because students have an overview of what they need to do at all times, they can also more easily work on the curriculum goals at a pace appropriate for them so that learning is adjusted to each individual. By allowing students to work at their own pace, one can challenge those who master their goals well while freeing up time to provide more support for those who need help. When writing about their learning journey on blogs, it is easy for the teachers to see what the students master.

Proper digital classroom management is not equal to the teacher having to be an expert on the use of digital technology. This book aims to get you up to speed on many of the tools out there. However, when you change the way you work in your classroom, you can take advantage of the students as experts as well. Do not get me

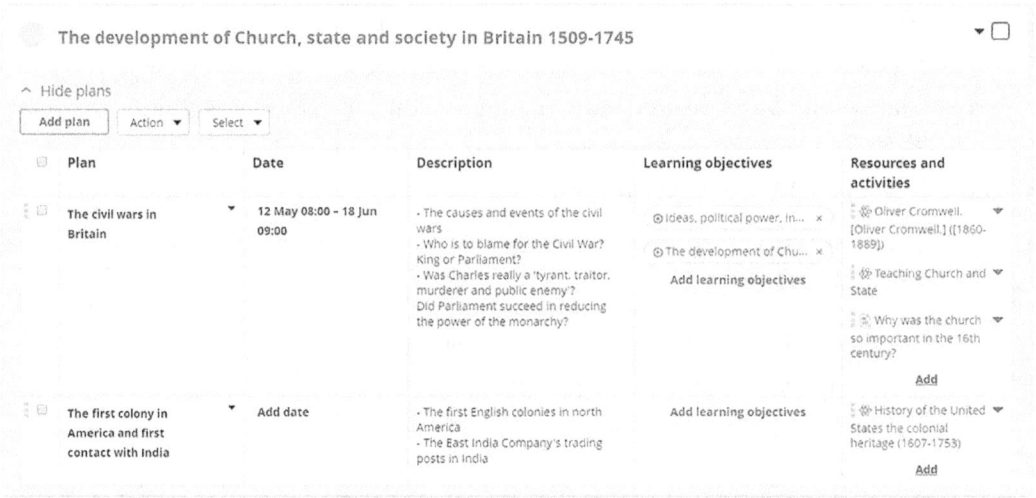

FIGURE 1.1 Learning objectives from the Learning Management Platform "It's Learning".

wrong; the teacher is still the most crucial part of the students' learning, in my opinion, but teaching needs to be changed from a teacher-focused classroom to a student lead environment. As described earlier, students in my class are active in figuring out how to reach their competency goals and in presenting what they master. When they have to make choices regarding managing information and communicating with students and experts outside the classroom, they gain a personal interest in success, and this creates engagement.

This student-centered approach also has implications for the assessments and feedback of students throughout the year. Here, of course, I distinguish between formative and summative assessment. Students should be able to suggest ways to show that they master a subject. This is in contrast to the traditional way, in which all students get the same test on the same day. We must challenge each student every day. You know you are successful if you can pick any student in your class, and they can tell you what they are learning, why it is important to learn it, and what their goal is that day. The learners need ownership of their learning, and you know they do when they are excited to tell you about it. The key takeaways are to meet the students where they are and move them as far and as fast as they can go. As for high schools, in particular, we are looking for agency in the students. They know what they want to pursue, not based on what they think is right but what they know they can accomplish. This is a process that should be going on throughout high school.

Most schools use a learning platform, where you can tie up curriculum goals with work tasks and assessment and put this into a weekly planner. That way, the teacher gets a good overview of which curriculum goals are covered, as does the student.

You can also do this with OneNote Class Notebooks (see Chapter 2).

In traditional schools, we have grades as a motivator, or what Daniel Pink calls the carrot-and-stick approach:

> Research by Carol Dweck and others has shown that there's a difference between learning goals and performance goals. A learning goal is, "I want to master

algebra." A performance goal is, "I want to get an A in algebra." The research shows that reaching performance goals doesn't necessarily mean that you have hit a learning goal. If people are single-mindedly focused on performance goals—and they achieve them—it doesn't mean they've learned anything, improved their capabilities, or mastered something complex. The kid is less likely to retain what she learned to get the A, less likely to persist when the going gets tough, and less likely to understand why algebra is important in the first place.

(Azzam, 2014)

However, if a kid is single-mindedly focused on a learning goal—mastering algebra—chances are he's going to do pretty well. In the process, he'll probably attain that performance goal and get his A. So it is best to simply go for the learning goal and use the grades and scores as feedback as the student works toward mastery (Azzam, 2014).

If you want to engage students, you have to let go on control and create the conditions in which they can tap into their own inner motivations.

In some classrooms, students' work of reward and punishment is dominated by a logic that "if you do this, this happens": Research shows that such external motivation has little long-term effect. Students who are paid for schoolwork are performing *under* their level of ability (Pink, 2001).

As students engage in assignments that they can choose and that they find genuinely interesting, they are willing to put a lot more effort into it. Also, I would argue that they work better when they feel ownership of what to do and understand why they need to do it.

An example of this is when 27 students and I wrote the book *Connected Learners, a Step-by-Step Guide to Creating a Global Classroom* (2013). A project that took 6 months, working hard 1 day a week during our English class. Participation was voluntary, and the students could pick any topic related to this way of learning. The most popular topic? Motivation, what motivates me in school. To reward those who contributed the most, we indexed the pages. A great way to visualize participation.

A global classroom with personal learning networks

An essential element in the new digital pedagogy we need in schools is that learning takes place in the same form as in the community outside. If students need answers, they might ask a friend on Snapchat or look it up on YouTube. The older generation also learns this way, through discussion forums and online instructional videos. You can immediately get answers to almost anything from experts in the field. By opening up the classroom and seeking support and collaborating with others, you are supporting this way of learning. The classroom becomes "global"; we open it up to the rest of the world by encouraging input from more than students, teachers, and textbook authors. In the global classroom, the whole world is supporting the students' learning.

The global classroom is also a good starting point for addressing the subject of reliable sources and who you can trust. This topic is discussed in Chapter 8. When you open the classroom to the rest of the world, the teacher becomes more important than ever.

The teacher needs a vast network; in fact, we can say that the teacher's learning is as essential as the students. When the teacher builds a network outside the classroom to make learning more relevant and exciting for the students, it also helps the teacher.

As an example, I can mention those in my network, many who are experts in education and learning using technology. The network helps me to stay up to date. I have contacts in many countries, and I often ask for help and advice. Sometimes I ask my network to participate in projects with my class, like when working on climate change described earlier.

In other words, I use the network both for my learning and for my students. I am not an expert in all areas, but I know how to ask for advice. No matter what you are teaching and what language you use to communicate, a network of teachers and experts will always be useful both to students and to the teacher. The next chapter shows you how you can start building your network.

IT STARTED WITH A TWITTER MESSAGE

When working with teenagers, it's important to keep up with what's happening within social media and technology. Now that we are all in touch with each other, it was natural for me to try to establish contacts all over the world. I teach English in high school, and I wanted to put my students in contact with students who spoke English. I sent out a tweet where I asked if any teachers were interested and waited for an answer. The answer came quickly! In the course of one day, I had contacted a school in Massachusetts. After some emails and Skype calls between me and my transatlantic colleague, we agreed on when our students could meet through Skype.

I discussed specific discussion topics with the teacher, and we divided the students into groups of four, with one computer per group. The students prepared questions beforehand, and the result was a success. My Norwegian students were very excited to have talked to peers in American high schools. The follow-up was a closed group on Facebook with more contact in the time that followed. Each time we "met" our new American friends, my students rejoiced. The exchange of questions and the answers we received is truly inspiring, and the American students appreciated this just as much as Norwegian my students.

Elaine Fleischer, teacher, Nadderud High School, Bekkestua, Norway

References

Azzam, A. M. (2014). Motivated to learn: A conversation with David Pink. *EL: Educational Leadership*, 72(1), 12–17. From EL: Educational Leadership: http://www.ascd.org/publications/educational-leadership/sept14/vol72/num01/Motivated-to-Learn@-A-Conversation-with-Daniel-Pink.aspx

Baker, J. C. (2006). *Schedule matters*. Seattle: Washington School Research Center.

Canady, R. L., & Rettig, M. D. (1996). *Teaching in the Blockblock: Strategies for engaging active learners*. Princeton, NJ: Eye of Education.

Fullan, M., & Langworthy, M. (2014). *A rich seam: How new pedagogies find deep learning*. London: Pearson.

Lynch, M. (2019, March 13). *What is the difference between deep learning and deeper learning?* From The Tech Edvocate: https://www.thetechedvocate.org/what-is-the-difference-between-deep-learning-and-deeper-learning/

McCoy, M. H. (1998). *Block scheduling: Does it make a difference? A high school case study.* From ERIC: https://eric.ed.gov/?id=ed420106

Michaelsen, A. S. (2013). *Connected learners: A step-by-guide to creating a global classroom.* Virgiania Beach, VA: Powerful Learning Practice Press.

Norway, Department of Education. (2016). *Meld. St.28*. Oslo, Norway: Det kongelige kunnskaps departement.

Pandolpho, B. (2019, February 20). *Reader idea: Helping students discover and write about the issues that matter to them.* From New York Times: https://www.nytimes.com/2019/02/20/learning/reader-idea-helping-students-discover-and-write-about-the-issues-that-matter-to-them.html?rref=collection%2Fsectioncollection%2Flesson-plans&action=click&contentCollection=lesson-plans&region=rank&module=package&version=highlights&contentPlacement=7&pgtype=sectionfront

Pink, D. (2001). *Drive: the surprising truth about what motivates us.* New York, NY: Penguin.

United Nations. (2019, July 16). *Sustainable development goals.* From United Nations Development Programme: https://www.undp.org/content/undp/en/home/sustainable-development-goals.html

Weingartner, N. P. (1969). *Teaching as a subversive activity.* New York, NY: Delta Books.

CHAPTER 2

Digital tools for the classroom

Ann S. Michaelsen

Introduction

This chapter presents a selection of tools that I believe are smart to use with students in the classroom. These are tools for individual work as well as for working in groups, and after introducing the tools, I give some examples of how to use them. Some are excellent to use when communicating and collaborating with people outside the classroom, the theme for the next chapter. I have tried to categorize the tools based on this system: searching and keeping track of information, writing and creating together, and, for students, showing what they have mastered. I need to stress that many of the tools can be used in multiple ways.

The collection of tools I present is limited; I'm only aiming at giving you an idea of what is available. Besides, tools will soon become outdated in a field that develops so quickly. Therefore, you must stay up to date through your network! I explain how you can establish a personal learning network in the next chapter.

Searching and keeping track of information

Most people spend a lot of time on Google searches; in fact, if you search for that data, you will find numbers around 2.5 hours a day. Is that true? I'm not sure, but it pays to know how to search accurately. Have you ever looked at all the results you get from a search and wondered if you should look beyond the three first entries? Do you take time to think about how you search? And do you talk to your students explaining how they search online? Everyone assumes they know how to; the question is, Do they?

Much of the learning in my class is based on research online. Most teachers will sooner or later ask their students to find information online. It is therefore vital that we prepare our students, because students need to know how to find reliable sources. In this section, we take a closer look at the use of Google, one of the most-used search engines. I show you ways to use Google search that you may not be familiar with.

I also comment on some alternative search engines and even more specific search tools. In Chapter 8, I take a closer look at verifying sources online.

Specific searches

A search can yield millions of results. How do you know that the top three results are the best? Do you scroll down to page 2 or page 3? Perhaps you could be more specific in your searches? Think about what keywords you're using. Using the exact phrase is often a good idea. Use quotation marks to start and end the phrase. "___" tells Google that you only want a precise phrase in the results. Try "Brexit what is happening?" and see what results you get.

Exclude terms with a minus sign. Not interested in Brexit? Try "BBC news − Brexit." No space after the minus. Ever forgotten a word or two from a specific phrase, song lyric, movie quote, or something else? You can use an asterisk (★) as a wildcard, which can help you find the missing word in a phrase.

By default, when you search, Google will include all the terms specified in the search. If you use multiple words in your search, the search application will give you results where all the words are included. It will be like saying, "I want this and also this." But you can also narrow your search by something called a Boolean Search. The Boolean operators are AND, OR, NOT, and NEAR. By default, when you search, Google will include all the terms specified in the search. If you're looking for one or more terms to match, then you can use a Boolean operator.

> AND +: "all words must be present in the results." OR "results can include any of the words." NOT −: "Results include everything but the term that follows the operator" (for example, diet NOT meat). NEAR: "The search terms must appear within a certain number of words of each other." Want to find something that looks like your favorite post? Use the search word **related**.
>
> Try this: related:Washingtonpost.com

Use quotation marks if you want to use exact phrases, not just searches based on one word. When you type a word or phrase between the two quotes, Google will only give you results where the exact words occur in the order in which you typed them. "London Bridge" only gives you text with London Bridge, while London Bridge gives you hits on both London and bridges separately.

Let's say you want to include a word in your search but also want to add results that contain similar words or synonyms. To do this, use the "~" in front of the word (Shah, 2019).

Searching a particular country or domain

Many times, it is smart to limit your search to a country or domain, for example, .ac or .us. ac stands for academic, and .us is the country code for the United States. You can also add the keyword "site" to narrow your search. Site means place, and by that, we mean the origin of the website. If you want to search in the United Kingdom, write site:uk. The endings .gov or .org are official channels or organizations. .edu stands

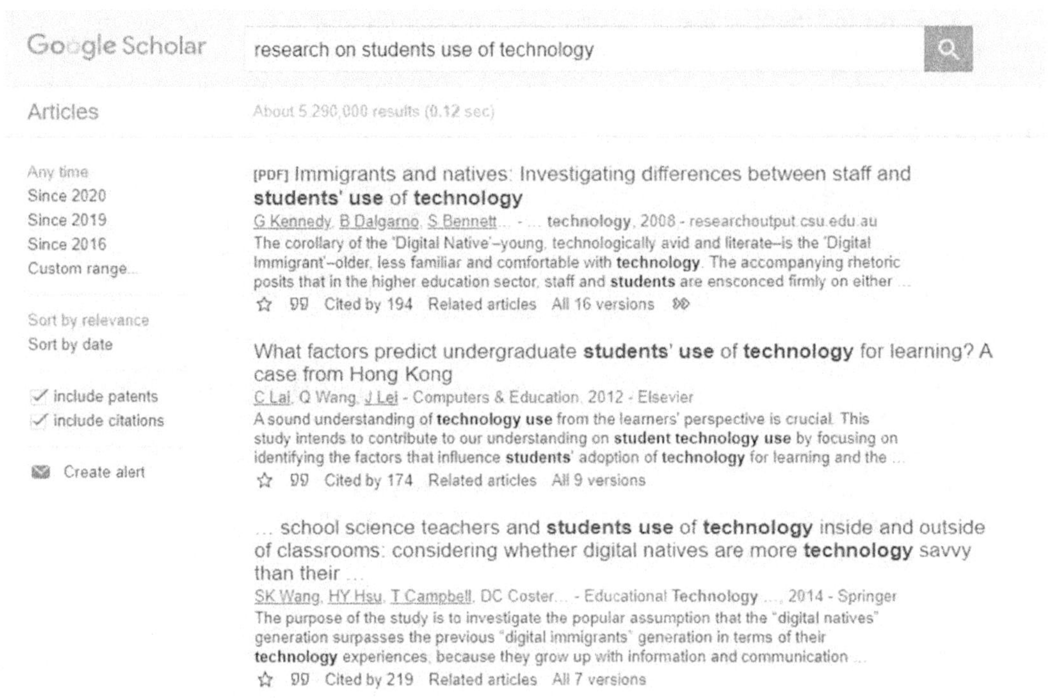

FIGURE 2.1 Results for Google Scholar search for students use of technology.

for education and is used in colleges and universities. If you're looking for articles on searching online for students, you can add the following search query: "Safe internet search for students" site:gov. The results you get are often thorough and reliable. To find scientific papers, visit Google Scholar. You find that when you search for academic articles. See Figure 2.1.

Alternative Search Engines

It is important to note that Google adapts the results to what you have previously searched for (see Chapter 7 for more on this). It is, therefore, sometimes a good idea to use other search engines. Give your students the task of testing the different options listed, which were the eight most popular search engines in 2019. Let all the students search for a specific topic and compare the results. The purpose of this is to show that there are alternatives to a simple search on Google. Everyone knows about Google and Bing, but are you familiar with these?

- Yahoo
- DuckDuckGo
- Baidu – 75 percent of the Chinese market
- Ask.com
- Startpage

- Yandex – Russian search engine
- Yippy Search
- Ecosia – this is like any other search engine, with one significant difference: it uses its profits to plant trees.

Another search tool, **Google Books**, allows you to search the 2 million books that have been scanned and made available to everyone, everything from some chapters to a full version.

Wolfram Alpha is a computational search engine (sometimes referred to as an "answer engine"). The interface looks similar to that of a regular search engine, but queries typed into the search box give answers to specific questions rather than listings of websites that may be relevant to the query. Ask the question, "What is …" (Rouse, 2019).

Social bookmarking with Diigo

When you search online, it is a good idea to find a way to organize the webpages you think are useful. This way, it will be easy for you to revisit. I recommend using a site like Diigo. You can save bookmarks, highlight text, and comment directly on any webpage. You can download Diigo onto your computer, phone, or tablet, and your favorite webpages are available to you wherever you go. Students can establish groups where they share bookmarks, highlights, and comments with other team members. If you use Chrome as your browser, you can add Diigo as an extension.

One advantage of Diigo is that you can annotate and collect the web by highlighting and adding sticky notes to webpages. Search includes a full-text search for the pages that are bookmarked. Diigo is a useful tool for processing and evaluating information and can be an excellent tool for collaboration between students and teachers. When you find an article you want to use, highlight what you think is central, and add your comments. There is a free version of Diigo that is easy to use. Try it out in class and discuss with your students how it could be a smart way for them to work with information.

Take notes using Liner

There are other tools than Diigo you can use to highlight text. Liner is an example of a tool that works well. It is an extension to the Chrome browser. Liner is more of a personal highlighting tool whereby you can easily collect your highlights, organize them, and share them on other social networks. You can keep your highlights private, or you could make it go public to let other users discover your highlights. It has good customization options with other service integrations like Pocket and Evernote (Macwan, 2016).

Classroom application

Liner is a useful tool if you find an article online and would like to highlight some quotes or paragraphs for your students or if you want to show them your comments. For example, you can "yellow out" and comment on something you think is essential in an article and share it with your students. Students can also use Liner to view each other's notes, like when working on a written assignment or group work. Liner is also suitable for individual feedback. If your students write blogs, you can use Liner for corrections and comments. Only the student you share this with will see it.

Annotating and writing together

Now I will introduce digital tools to use for brainstorming, co-writing, and sharing – between you and your students, among students, and between students in your class and the outside world. The point of using these tools is to facilitate an interaction between learners by making it easier to exchange ideas and work together with different types of text creation. The tools can be used as a topic starter: What do you already know? Then you make sure all ideas are shared and saved. It is a good idea to look at these afterward, pointing out what we know now.

Start thought processes with EdWordle

EdWordle is a tool for editing "word clouds" based on Wordle. You can re-font, recolor, resize, move, rotate, add, and delete words to create custom visualizations.

It is easy to create a word cloud. You enter the ewordle.net and press "*Create now.*" You'll get a text box where you type the words or paragraphs you want to use in your word cloud. EdWordle automatically removes interjections like *and*, *it*, and *oh*.

Once you've pressed "*Create a wordle,*" you'll get your cloud, along with a toolbar you can use to change the language, font and size, color, appearance, and position of the words. Another exciting feature of edWordle is the "*Re-Layout*" button. By tapping it, you can bring up variations of the text you've used. See an example in Figure 2.2.

FIGURE 2.2 An EDWordle made from keywords in this chapter.

Classroom application

After creating the word cloud, you can print it out or save it on your PC and share it with others. Use EdWordle to brainstorm before a new topic to see what students already know. Ask students to share keywords and display the result on a projector in class. Make a word cloud before and after reviewing a new topic. The advantage of doing this online and not on paper is that you can save it and use it when revisiting the topic before a test or an exam.

Use Padlet for idea development and notes

Padlet is an online bulletin board where students and teachers can collaborate, reflect, share links, and pictures.

Padlet is great for gathering ideas, sharing them, and modifying them later. Users can add links, YouTube videos, files, and images.

Choose "*Make a Padlet*," and you'll get a wall where you can start writing. You can add images and files straight into your Padlet. Once you're logged in, you can access the Padlets you've created and edit them.

You can share your Padlet on social media or with your learning platform; just click "*Share*" and choose where you want to share it. For example, you can create a mind map and use it as a brainstorming exercise when working on a new theme or as repetition. You can share videos, bookmarks, webpages, and more. For students to find facts about a topic, you can create a wall and share it with students. Students can also type the information they have gathered into a mutual document, get inspiration, and learn more by reading what the other students have written.

Using Talkwall when particpants are at different locations

Talkwall is a similar product to Padlet a tool developed at the University in Oslo. It is based on microblogging and visualization of conversations and can help students to have better dialogues in the classroom. Talkwall is a tool developed to support learning through exploratory talk. Exploratory talk is characterized by everyone contributing views, opinions, and reasons.

Classroom application

Both Padlet and Talkwall are virtual "bulletin" boards where students and teachers can collaborate, reflect, and share links and pictures. You, as a teacher, can create a bulletin board and share the address with your students. The students can write either in groups or alone. It is also an excellent way to collaborate outside the classroom. I have used this many times when working on projects in which we have invited students from other countries. An example of a Padlet used with my students is found in Figure 2.3.

Mind maps

Mind mapping can help students organize ideas and make sense of the material. There are a lot of different ways to use a mindmap in class. When visualizing what they are

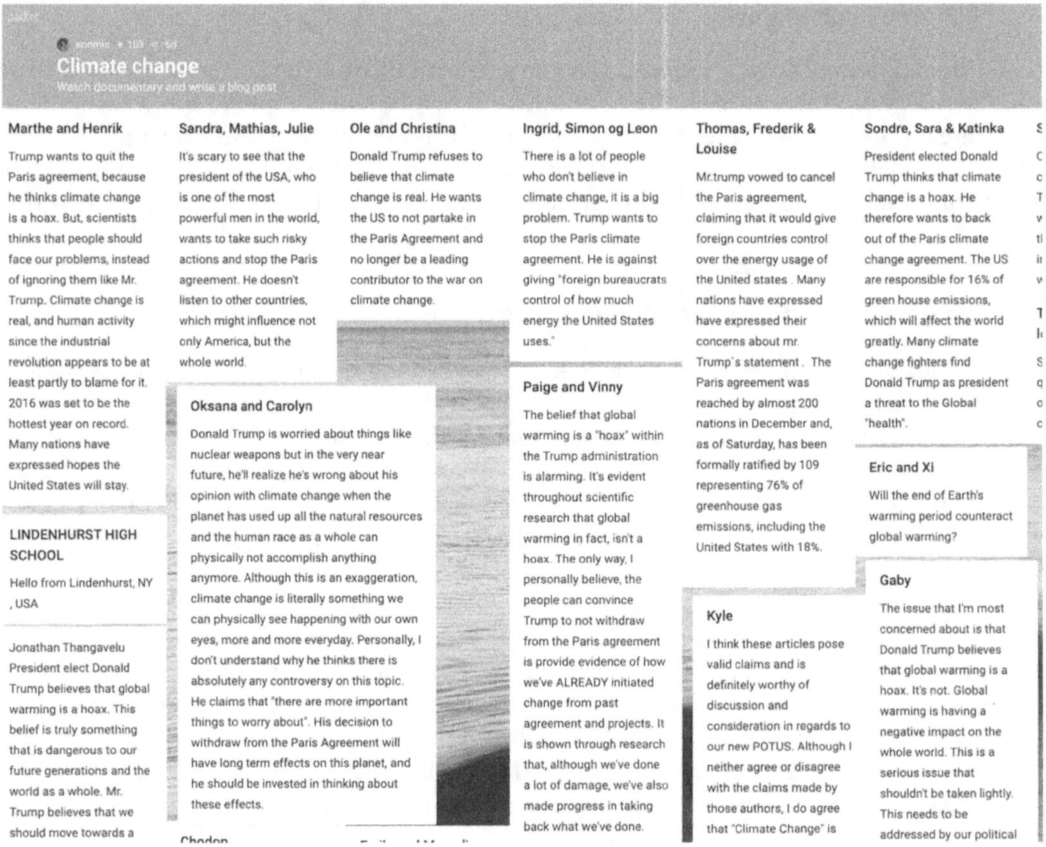

FIGURE 2.3 A Padlet where students share information about climate change.

learning, students get a chance to question. Asking questions is a good way for students to learn. Intellectual curiosity, referring to students' motivation to comprehend and engage in cognitively demanding tasks, is identified as a third major predictor of success in academic performance, after intelligence and effort. Studies have shown that this kind of questioning is rarely observed in classroom and that teachers need help to find good ways to do this. Mind maps can be used to (a) define and visualize curriculum objectives, (b) elicit prior student knowledge, (c) generate and discuss student questions, (d) guide collective knowledge construction, and (e) monitor and evaluate the development of both individual and collective knowledge (Stokhof, Stokhof, Vries, Bastiaens, & Martens, 2018).

Classroom application

Start any new topic with a mind map and start with what the students already know about the topic. Have the students ask questions; then they have to think about what they believe they need to know. It is an excellent way to reflect on prior knowledge. Areas in which mind maps are helpful are revision, presentations, and group assignments, where students can collaborate working on a mind map. See the following list of online mind-map apps.

Apps for making mind maps

Coggle is an online tool for creating and sharing mind maps and flow charts. It works online in your browser: no need to download or install. It is useful for taking notes, brainstorming, planning, or doing something creative; it is simple to visualize your ideas.

SimpleMind is a mind-mapping solution that simplifies the process of structuring, analyzing, and presenting thoughts. It has a free-form layout feature that allows users to organize their thoughts and arrange topics precisely the way they want.

MindMup is an easy-to-use web-based mind-mapping software that requires no signup for users. It enables users to save files online, share them with others, or export them to other mediums.

Sharing notes with OneNote

OneNote is a digital notebook that is included in Microsoft Office, together with Word, Excel, and PowerPoint. In Norway, all schools at the high school level have access to Office 365. Both teachers and students can download OneNote to multiple devices.

When you start up OneNote, you'll be able to select a new notebook and choose whether to save it online or locally on your computer. The advantage of saving it online is that you can access it from anywhere, on any computer, phone, or tablet.

OneNote organizes the notebook into sections and pages. The pages have no restrictions, and you can add as many pictures, text boxes, and other items as you want. Screenshots, videos, and audio are easily inserted into your notes, and you can even record yourself. Choosing "*Record video*" will give you both audio and video. It is also possible to create illustrations with the built-in drawing function, which is smart to use with mind maps. OneNote is also closely associated with the other software in the Office family. You can easily insert an Excel worksheet directly into your notes.

Everything you type is automatically saved, you do not have to remember to save it, and you can effortlessly search your notes. The search engine is so refined that it recognizes text in images. Images of old news articles are also searchable. The same applies to audio and video files. Every time you write something important, you can click on the appropriate tag. A tag is like a sticky note. Examples are "to do," "important," "with a star," "question" for further work, and so on. You can also create your personalized tags. When going back on notes to review before an exam, for instance, you can search for all your tags. As an example, students can take notes and use presentations from the teacher, and when studying for a test, they can use the tags to be sure they find everything they need. Students can use the code exam, and they will then, with a quick search, get a list of all that is important to know as an alternative to searching with specific keywords.

If you are using Office 356, OneNote will be associated with your site on the Microsoft cloud OneDrive (discussed later). Your notes will then be saved "in the cloud" so that they are accessible from all kinds of devices through the Office web applications. You don't need a computer with OneNote installed but can read through your notes on your phone or tablet anywhere.

OneNote also has a useful feature called OneNote Class notebook. It is easy to create by selecting the option in Office 365. When you create a Class notebook, you can add other teachers before you add students. Once all students are added to the notebook, you can start adding content. Many teachers use class notebooks to read and assess assignments, distribute materials to students, and allow students to co-write. A Class notebook consists of two parts. One part is accessible to everyone, students and teachers, and it can be used for class material. The second part is private for each student, and has an area in the notebook only shared with the teacher. This area is often divided into multiple tabs that you name when you create the OneNote Class notebook. You will also find a function called "*Distribute Page*." Here you can easily share documents with each student. You can also use the "*Review student work*" feature to correct tasks students submit in the Class notebook.

Classroom application

Each student can use OneNote as a personal note-taking tool to organize material in preparation for an assessment or homework. The teacher can also use OneNote to share content with the students. However, the best learning with OneNote happens when students share notes. That is the main reason why I recommend that teachers use a OneNote Class notebook. Students download the notebook on their computers, and in Norway, they can use it during all the written exams. In other words, it is a collaborative space where students can help each other and where the teacher can share useful information.

Because OneNote is connected to the Microsoft cloud, any changes you make will be stored in the cloud and on your PC. When you work offline, you get the version you have on your computer. Each time you connect to the web, OneNote will search for updates. This means that when many students log on at the same time, their notebooks will be updated. Should many write at the same time, the program will tell you if there is a conflict, and then you can choose which version you want to use. In other words, students can correct, post, and share.

Another feature of OneNote that many of the teachers at my school like is the way you can comment on students' work. If you're correcting an assignment, you can write and speak at the same time – just tap in the document where you want to add an audio/video note and start recording. Then select "*Play video*" from the menu to view. Many students prefer to hear their teacher instead of traditional written feedback. Some teachers might worry that it is time-consuming, but the benefits seem to be worth it. In other words, OneNote supports both audio and video, and it is easy to use this feature. Students can also easily record their work or presentations to the teacher – an alternative to students presenting in class.

Share documents with Dropbox

Dropbox is a service for storing documents online. It is a smart place to share files typically when working on a project with someone outside your organization. You download the software on your computer and find it in your file folder. It is easy to use and a smart solution if the files you are sharing are too large to send in an email.

All you need is access to the web, and you can use your files in the same way as if they were on your computer, mobile, or tablet. Dropbox is easy to use, and there is a free version that's perfect to use for projects with students.

To use Dropbox, you need to download the software and install it on your computer. All students who are administrators on their machines can easily do this. Dropbox creates a folder for you. You get 2 GB of storage for free, and you can use any PC, tablet, or smartphone to access Dropbox. Many think Dropbox is smart as a supplement to Office 365 because you can share documents with everyone, also those who do not have a Microsoft Office license.

Classroom application

The free version has limited space. However, that should not be a problem because this is supposed to be used as a temporary storage place. You "drop" your files where others can easily retrieve them. By selecting "*Share*" from the Dropbox site, you can share a folder. Users will then be notified. When the project is over, you delete the files or move them to another permanent place on your computer.

Consequently, Dropbox is ideal for sharing documents with multiple writers. Students who work with a task should always use a cloud storage service so that everyone has access to the documents. When the project is over, they can move the documents to free up space for new projects. Ever had students claim they left their work on another computer? Isn't it annoying that when working in groups, it always seems that it is the absent student who has the material on their computer? No longer; in a digital classroom, this should not be an obstacle.

Write together and share files with Google Docs/Google Drive

Google has Google Docs and a cloud storage system – Google Drive. You get 15 GB of storage as well as Google Docs, Google Sheets, Google Slides, and Google mail; if you need more storage, you have to pay. Documents you create in Google Docs will be stored in the Google Drive cloud storage service. Unlike Dropbox, Google Drive lets you open over 30 different file types right in your browser. You do not need to install anything on your computer, meaning that you can make changes to a PowerPoint presentation even if you don't have Office installed on the device. You simply choose "*Open with Google Slides.*" We have used this when students and I have presented together at conferences. Then we can separately add slides and comments. You can also write and edit your documents when you're online. In other words, just as with Office 356, this is a brilliant way to work in teams and on projects in school. You can also use the comment box at the top right to discuss with the group and find out what they think about the changes. Even if you are offline, you will have the latest version saved online in your browser if you use Google Chrome. It might be worth downloading Google Drive to your computer. Then all the folders you create in the cloud will appear locally on your computer. Everything you do in the documents on your computer is updated in the cloud when you're connected to the web.

Google Drive also allows you to search all your files at once, both those you have left on the web and those located on your computer. You can search by keyword and filter by file, author, and more. Google Drive can even recognize keywords in images and scanned documents.

Classroom application

Group work can be complicated if each student has the documents they are working on on their computer. With Google Drive, they can easily share all their documents. The advantage is that everyone has access, even if one student in the group is absent.

When you share files with Google, you can choose to share with others through a link or by entering the names of the people you want to work with, you can also share a link that allows them to read the file only, not modify it. It is essential that you tick the checkbox for them to edit.

One advantage of using Google in teamwork is that you can update files while you work. No need to send a document back and forth, everyone writes in the same document, and there is no confusion with which version was last updated. When you change a document, anyone with access can automatically see the changes as soon as you do them. In other words, multiple students can type in the same document at the same time. It works well when students work in small groups. With a whole class, it can be a little complicated.

Work in the cloud with OneDrive/Office 365

Not everyone knows that users of the Office 365 version get 1 TB of storage in the Microsoft cloud-hosting service OneDrive. Unlike Google Drive, which is free, many schools in Norway have bought Office 365 for their teachers and students.

One terabyte is two to three times the amount of space most new PCs are equipped with, so there is plenty of room for both schoolwork and entertainment if that is allowed on a school computer. In addition to storing files in OneDrive, it's possible to share files with other users so that they can view or edit them.

You can also edit documents stored in your OneDrive in your web browser. In other words, you can edit without having to open an Office program. Also, you use it with any device that's connected to the web.

To get started, go to OneDrive.com, sign in, and click "*Upload.*" Pick documents that you want to be able to share or be able to access on any computer.

You can use any computer with web access and view or edit the files stored on OneDrive. Many schools have their own login locations to access their software and documents when they are stored in Office 365. In other words, even if you're on a computer without the Microsoft Office suite, you can edit your document.

Classroom application

Dropbox, Google Drive, and OneDrive are the most commonly used cloud services in schools, at least in Norway. All three offer ways to store and share documents. A survey in Norway from 2016 rated Google Drive as the best cloud service, since it is easy to store, open, use, and share documents with a variety of platforms (Singsaas, 2016). Since most schools in Norway have Office 365 or are about to get Office 365, I still believe that it is a logical first choice. There's plenty of storage space there, and it's a safe and secure way to share documents. The reason I have chosen to review the other two options here is that they are all good, and the free versions are, in many cases, the only option. After using all three for several years, I cannot say that any of them are easier to use than the others. In many schools, I am guessing the decision has already been made.

Demonstrating mastery

In most of the preceding examples, students can demonstrate how they master the content. Here I show you some other tools that are useful both in written and oral assignments. Students learn a lot from getting constructive feedback, and these tools are excellent for both formative and summative assessments.

Empowering students through blogging

Written assignments are most often a Word file submitted in a learning management platform or, as mentioned, written in OneNote in the form of an OneNote Class notebook. Getting feedback from the teacher is helpful; peer review even better. It is also a good idea to get a wider audience for your students. A blog is a collection of writing and can be compared to a portfolio. See Chapter 3 for how students can set up their blogs as well as how you can too.

I usually list my students' blogs on my webpage as well as set up an RSS feed (also explained in Chapter 3). Then you will see when students post new entries on their blogs. When you list their blogs on your blog, you can share with your network. It is a perfect way to promote your students' work, helping them to get more readers and more feedback. School blogs do not get a wide audience unless you help promote them. If students are reluctant to share, the blogs can be password-protect. So far, I have never had any students do this.

Blogs to improve writing skills

My experience of using blogs with students is that it improves their writing skills. There are many reasons for this. I have found that they write longer text and, in general, write more often. A study (Azam, 2011) from 2010/2011 found that students' ability in producing recount text had improved, along with the changes in a classroom situation, which became more motivating. The improvement in students' writing skills includes (1) the students had fewer misspelled words in their writings, (2) the students used the words in their appropriate context, (3) they produced grammatically correct sentences related to recount text, (4) the students also could write the text chronologically, and (5) they are able to develop the text into interesting one (Azam, 2011).

Providing feedback for your students is an excellent way for them to learn. Try to make a routine of students reading each other's blogs and comment regularly. Students learn from seeing how their classmates have solved the same task. I always stress how important it is to receive good feedback from others on what they have written and that they need to learn how to write good comments. One apparent reason is that only by writing a detailed comment will the recipient know that they read the post. Most often, students will write comments like "wonderful" or "you are so smart." We need to know if they understood the content and if they have anything to offer to make it better. Students can offer advice on; should they have phrased the text differently? Did they get their point through, and were they convincing? What could they do in order to improve the blog post?

	Advanced	Proficient	Developing	Emerging
Quality of writing				
Content				
Use of sources				
Grammar, usage				

When working on writing good comments, it is a good idea to use a rubric, such as the one shown. That way, everyone knows what a good blog post looks like. That makes it easier for the students, even those who are on the beginner level. A smart way to start writing your blog posts is to get help from your classmates. I use peer assessment and will explain how that works here.

You can also use a single-point rubric that outlines the standards a student has to meet, leaving the categories concerns (areas that need work) and beyond expectations open.

Peer assessment

Some learning management systems offer anonymous peer assessment. That is a smart way to start off writing blogs. Everyone gets feedback from two or more students before they post their blogs. My students like this way of learning. There has been a lot of research on the area of peer assessment. The research supports my view on why this is important.

> Peer assessment is an effective classroom technique for improving academic performance. The results indicate that peer assessment can be effective across a wide range of subject areas, education levels, and assessment types. If used correctly, peer assessment can free up time for the teacher to assist students with greater difficulties or for more complex tasks. Anonymity is important because assessors are more likely, to be honest in their feedback, and interpersonal processes cannot influence how assessees receive the assessment feedback.
> (McGrane & Hopfenbeck, 2019; see Figure 2.4)

What I found was that the teacher needs to spend time on explaining what to assess and how to assess. You also have to model what a right answer looks like by going through the specific requirements for the assignment. It is an excellent way to see if your students understood the instructions and goals for the tasks. Research has also found that it is the feedback that is important, not the grading. Look at Figure 2.5 for an example of how to use a rubric when assessing the assignment.

> Modeling or training should be provided prior to or during the task because peer assessment is not easy. Teachers should ask students to be specific in their

feedback, particularly with regard to the problems in assessees' work, and to provide suggestions. The findings of our study could assist teachers in developing strategies to amplify the effectiveness of peer assessment for all students. Students should be encouraged to give thoughtful and meaningful comments rather than simply assign grades to peers. Students can be asked to explain why they assigned particular grades to peers. Third, teachers should scaffold assessment processes with scaffolding tools, particularly for the weak. Students should be encouraged to exchange affective comments that give socio-emotional support to peers and recognize peers' achievement. Our results suggest that positive affective comments are not just about making other people feel good. They can help boost the motivation, interest, and self-efficacy of assessees, which in turn can enhance their performance.

(Lu & Law, 2012)

If you want your students to receive more feedback, you can also organize with other teachers to get their students to comment. You can find teachers to collaborate with online through your personal learning network (see Chapter 3), but you can also get organized help. Quadblogging is a website established by a teacher in England, David Mitchell – @DeputyMitchell. The idea behind it is to help teachers find partners. After you sign up, you are put in groups with three other teachers. This happens twice a year. It's easy to get started. Enter the site quadblogging.com and register on the site.

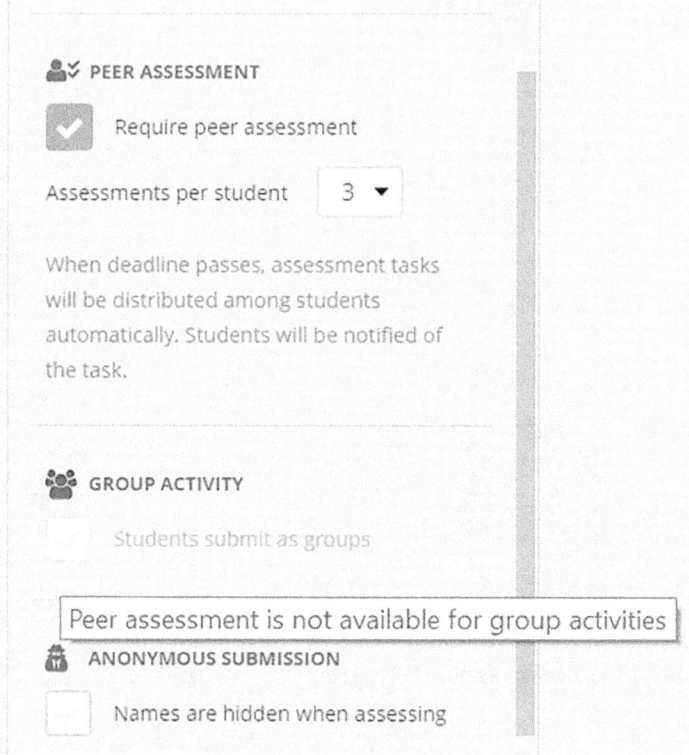

FIGURE 2.4 An example of peer assessment in the LMS its learning.

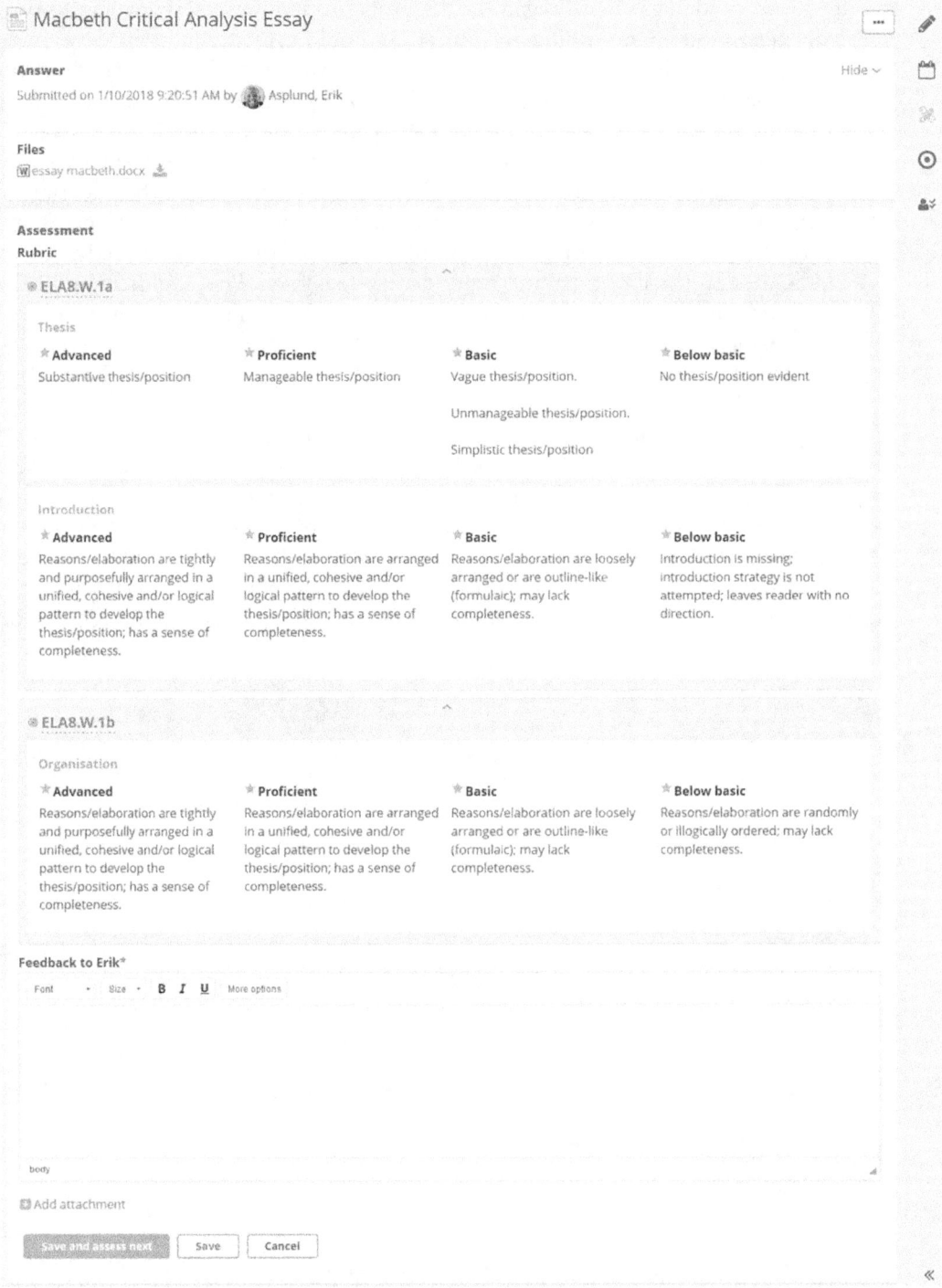

FIGURE 2.5 Assessment using a rubric with the LMS its learning.

I've used Quadblogging twice and think it's a great way to get in touch with other educators. In 2013, we worked with one school in the United States, one in Johannesburg, and one in England. In other words, we were four teachers who collaborated. That way, you can be sure that all your students get comments on their work.

Classroom application

Writing a blog is an integral part of how I work with my students. The content is determined by the competency goals. I find that most students like writing blogs and that they write a lot when they find the tasks relevant and interesting. They also show more precise work in terms of finding reliable sources, and they are more critical to what they post. Why is this? Most likely because they are motivated by knowing that they are writing for an authentic audience. In addition to the teacher, other students in the class can read the blog, and with help from the teacher, they can have a wider audience around the world.

A few simple steps to improve students' writing:

1. **Spelling and grammar errors** should be avoided! I advise students to write their texts in Word or OneNote and then paste them into the blog after they have used the spell check. If not, they can use the spell checker in their browser. I use the spell checker extension in Google Chrome. There are many dictionaries for English; Grammarly, a grammar checker, is also a great choice. I use Grammarly when I write in English, and my students do too. When working with foreign languages, there are many choices in software to use, and if you use Word, you will find most languages there.

   > Some writing advice applies to pretty much all situations. Try to spell everything right; use punctuation correctly, etc. But the best way to handle other qualities of your writing, like style and formality level, will vary depending on your situation. When you set your goals for a particular piece of writing, Grammarly can offer tailored writing suggestions that take your audience and writing style into account. Read on to find out what Grammarly takes into account when customizing your writing feedback.
   >
   > (Grammarly, 2020)

2. **Peer assessment.** I have already mentioned that I think it is a good idea for students to read and comment on each other's blog posts. In addition to that, it is smart to have them assess each other's work before they publish it. To do this, you have to make sure that the work is anonymous. Many learning management platforms offer this. We have been using itslearning at my school. When you assign a task for your students, you can choose peer assessment and choose a specific number of assessments per student. I usually choose three.

3. **Find images, text, and videos you can reuse.** Not all students know how to search for images they are licensed for reuse. When you do a Google search, you can filter your results to find images, videos, or text that you have permission to

use. To do this, use an Advanced Search filter called "*Usage rights*" that lets you know when you can use, share, or modify something you find online (Google Search Help, 2019). Wikimedia Commons is a great place to find images, audio, and video that can be used on a blog. Flickr and Creative Commons are other examples.

Check your knowledge with Kahoot!

Kahoot! is a tool for using technology to administer quizzes, discussions, or surveys. It is a game-based classroom response system played by the whole class in real time. Multiple-choice questions can be shown on the screen. Students answer questions with their smartphone, tablet, or computer. The goal is to make learning more inspiring and engaging for students while giving the teacher feedback on what the students know about any given subject. The competition element makes it more enjoyable than an ordinary test while the teacher can verify if the fact knowledge is there. It's easy to use, and students can use their phone to respond if they don't have their own PC or tablet. They need internet access; that is all.

Classroom application

In addition to being an entertaining way to test knowledge, Kahoot can be used for repetition before a test. The teacher can also use it to see what the students know about a topic before it is introduced. You can use the Kahoot app to assign quizzes for kids to complete at home, whether as homework or just for fun. Kahoot calls these anytime, anywhere quizzes "challenges." Teachers can assign them using the Kahoot website or app.

Students can even create a survey in Kahoot after they have worked on a topic that they can use with the class to see if they have paid attention to a presentation, for instance. By creating a Kahoot, students can demonstrate their expertise on the subject – the teacher can quickly tell by the questions and answers. Student participation is an important factor in promoting students' motivation for learning, and the best learning effect is when students get to ask the questions. Students become active performers in their learning, and it is a good way to check for understanding. There are also a lot of ready-made quizzes to use.

Record student presentations

Audio and video recording can also be used to promote learning. In this section, we take a look at some of the tools you or your students can use to record presentations. Most of the software I discuss here can be used by teachers when they make videos for the flipped classroom. Look for more information on the flipped classroom in Chapter 6. It is smart to have your students make videos too. Both can be used by the students to learn and for the students to show that they master the content.

In most cases, the camera on your mobile phone works well enough for recording. If you are using a computer, it may be a good idea to use an external microphone that connects to a USB port. You get so much better sound with an external microphone.

A more advanced recording software that is hosted on the web and recommended by teachers at my school is the Screencast-O-Matic. Screencast-O-Matic is a video-editing software tool that can be launched directly from a browser. Use it when making flipped classroom videos; students can also use it when they make videos as assignments.

Screencast-O-Matic has a free version that is sufficient for most – the maximum recording time is 15 minutes. Practice before you make a video to share with your class. Be sure to visit the website, which has many tutorials for you.

Another good option is Camtasia Studio. Camtasia is a software for creating video tutorials and presentations or via a direct recording plug-in to Microsoft PowerPoint.

Many teachers use this for the flipped classroom (see Chapter 6), and it can also be used for making recordings in the classroom. They offer a free trial version, so try that before you spend money on it.

However, did you know that you can make a video with PowerPoint? You might remember Office Mix, a separate add-on in Office 365. PowerPoint now has another version, and you'll find the feature in *"Slide Show."* You can create a video of your presentation and post it online or share it directly with your students. Then they can watch the video of your presentation as many times as they want/need. If you choose *"Record slideshow,"* you make a recording of your PowerPoint presentation, and students will see you in the corner of the presentation. It's nice to use when you need to explain something to your students.

On a Mac, you can use QuickTime Player to record your screen outside of PowerPoint. It might be useful if you want to show something on a webpage or perhaps a software program that you want to explain. It's easy to figure out how to do this. In the QuickTime Player application on your Mac, choose *File > New screen capture*.

Classroom application

Whenever a student holds a presentation in front of the class, it can become a challenge for the teacher to assess it accurately, and with 30 students in each class, it takes time. In Norway, this is a very common way for students to show they have mastered a particular content area. To save time, it is a good idea to record/record your students' presentations and then watch or listen to them later.

You can capture your presentation while the students perform in front of the class, but you can also let students prerecord their presentations at home. This is great for students who do not like to stand in front of the class. Just be sure that they are not reading from a manuscript and that you take time to questions them on the topic later.

Learning with podcasts

Podcasts are popular, and many people subscribe to podcasts. There are may ways to subscribe to podcasts, and many that can be used in class; one example is "The Daily," from the *New York Times*, a 20-minute podcast made every day. Lifewire has a list of great podcasts to use in class. Its slogan is "Want more facts and less commentary? Listen up." It is a great way to keep up to date because you can download them and listen to them in the car or when you go hiking. The only thing you have to do is download an app on your phone, find some interesting podcasts to subscribe to, and then you are good to go (Stephenson, 2020).

Creating a podcast is also a great way for students to share their knowledge. I have read many posts on how students learn more when they teach others. Students, when working on assignments, come up with interesting questions, do the research, and present the result to the rest of the class. This is an excellent way to learn, for teachers and students. This way of working is common in schools in Norway. I'm not sure how many use podcasts, but I know it has great potential.

> The real power of narrative podcasts lies in the effect that storytelling has on retention. Stories are the foundation of how we understand and remember information. They do this by triggering our emotions and tying information to the way we feel when we learn something new. By intertwining content with a story, learners are better equipped to recall information by recalling the way they felt when they learned the information. According to the London School of Business, learners retain facts at only a rate of about 5 to 10 percent. Tying these facts to images can help increase retention up to 25 percent. However, if facts and concepts are interwoven into stories, retention levels can reach as high as 65 to 75 percent. Narrative podcasts present an excellent opportunity to increase learner retention levels without much need for monetary investments or specialized skill sets.
>
> (D'Anza, 2018)

Classroom application

What I do is assign different topics to the students before the exam and have them make videos or podcasts to share with the rest of the class. If you introduce making a podcast at the start of the semester, they will know how to do it. An interview makes for an exciting podcast; students need to come up with interesting and useful questions. Also, they need an introduction so that listeners know what is coming. There are many podcasts you can listen to with your students, and then you can discuss what works well. The length of the podcast is also an issue. Not too long, not too short!

To make podcasts, you need a phone and software to record. There are many to choose from. Audacity is one. Audacity is a free and open-source digital audio editor and recording application software available for Windows, MacOS/OS X, and Unix-like operating systems.

You can also use the normal recording function of your phone.

Learning online

If students are unable to attend school for any reason, there are many ways to meet the students online. During the first outbreak of the COVID-19 virus in 2020, that was the norm for most students in the world. Many teachers invited their students into a digital classroom via Microsoft Teams or Zoom. I'm sure there were other platforms used as well, but as far as I know, these were the most popular among educators in Norway.

During the spring of 2020, a lot of software was free for schools. That meant teachers could choose from a wide range of software and content online. Online learning is a different way to both teach and learn. Either way, if you use Microsoft Teams or Zoom, it is essential to plan the lessons just like you would in a traditional classroom, opening for new ways for assessing student work.

Classroom application

After working in a distance learning classroom several months, many teachers see advantages of this new way of teaching and learning. Students who are unable to attend school for some reason can still participate in class activities. If the teachers set up their computer with videoconferencing software, students can log in from home and actively participate. In this mixed environment, you can have some students at school and some at home online at the same time. If you use the pedagogy that I have described in this book, students can meet at the start of the day for instructions and clarifications. They can continue working alone or in teams, virtually or at school. When teaching online, it is a good idea to **keep** your talking to a minimum. Instructional videos can be shared with the students to watch at their convenience. If you want to share a PowerPoint presentation, have your headshot at the corner of the screen. Remember, the tasks should be engaging and inclusive, relevant, and meaningful. Create small groups to encourage group discussions and have students pose questions in the chat panel. Use technology creatively.

References

Azam, N. A. (2011). *Utilizing student blogs to improve writing skills (an action research at 8th grade of SMP Negeri 1 Wonogiri in the academic year of 2010/2011)*. From Semantic Scholar: https://eprints.uns.ac.id/10193

D'Anza, J. (2018, June 31). *Learning solution*. From What Are Narrative Podcasts? Why Use Them in eLearning? https://learningsolutionsmag.com/articles/what-are-narrative-podcasts-why-use-them-in-elearning

Google Search Help. (2019). *From find free-to-use images*. From https://support.google.com/websearch/answer/29508?hl=en

Grammarly. (2020, January 10). *How to set goals in the Grammarly editor, and why you should*. From Grammarly Spotlight: https://www.grammarly.com/blog/set-goals-grammarly-editor/

Lu, J., & Law, N. (2012). *Online peer assessment: Effects of cognitive and affective feedback*. From Springer Link: https://link.springer.com/article/10.1007/s11251-011-9177-2

Macwan, A. (2016, July 28). *Highly vs Liner vs Marker: Highlighting text & sharing*. From Guiding Tech: https://www.guidingtech.com/60603/highly-vs-liner-vs-marker-highlight/

McGrane, J. A., & Hopfenbeck, T. N. (2019). *The impact of peer assessment on academic performance: A meta-analysis of control group studies*. London: Springer Link.

Rouse, M. (2019). *What is Wolfram Alpha?* From Whatis.techtarget.com: https://whatis.techtarget.com/definition/Wolfram-Alpha

Shah, D. (2019, April 3). *Think you know how to search with Google? Think again*. From Entrepreneurs Organization: https://blog.eonetwork.org/2019/04/think-know-search-google-think-31-google-advanced-search-tips/

Singsaas, F. (2016, February 11). *Hvilken skylagringstjeneste er best?* [Which cloud storage is best?]. From Aftenposten: https://www.aftenposten.no/digital/i/b58Rjl/hvilken-skylagringstjeneste-er-best

Stephenson, B. (2020, February 24). *The 12 best news podcasts of 2020.* From Lifewire: https://www.lifewire.com/best-news-podcasts-4171518

Stokhof, H., Stokhof, H., Vries, B. D., Bastiaens, T., & Martens, R. (2018). Using mind maps to make student questioning effective: Learning outcomes of a principle-based scenario for teacher guidance. *Research in Science Education*, 2018, 1–23.

CHAPTER 3

Social media in the global classroom

Ann S. Michaelsen

Introduction

Communication and interaction are essential parts of learning. In a traditional classroom, teachers and students interact, but with the use of technology, we can communicate with people outside our classroom. Social media can help you.

There are many areas in which social media can be useful in students' learning: language skills, interpersonal skills, learning about cultural differences – the list is long. How about finding a class in Europe to practice your French? When learning about world religions, how about discussing with people from different parts of the world? In this chapter, we look into a range of social media and how we can use it to communicate outside the classroom – transforming the way we learn.

Twitter as a source of information

The Twitter micro-blog service, founded in San Francisco in 2006, currently has hundreds of millions of users. The website is a popular channel for communication between individuals worldwide, politicians, business leaders, and media people; many are avid users. You can use Twitter to connect with people from around the world, stay updated on important topics, and participate in discussions. Twitter is often used by teachers to keep up on content, technology, and pedagogy. You can use Twitter when you have a question about something professional or want updates on the latest news.

The first thing to do is to find someone you want to follow. That could be teachers at your school, people speaking at conferences, or experts in different fields. The easiest way to find people on Twitter is to Google the name of the person, followed by the word *Twitter* or "on Twitter." If you find people that you think are contributing in a positive and informative way, it's good advice to see who they follow and then follow them too.

You can also participate by writing "tweets," sharing photos and websites, in short networking. To send a tweet, you must click "*Write new Tweet*" and remember that what you're typing may not be longer than 280 characters. You might have heard that you can only write 140 characters, but Twitter doubled the number in 2017. You can invite others to join in a conversation by typing @ and then their Twitter name, for example, @annmic = Ann S. Michaelsen. You can answer or ask questions. The possibilities are endless. My experience is that many are willing to contribute to projects with teachers and students. See the examples later in this chapter.

When you start with Twitter, very few people will follow you. Maybe you get about 50 followers in the beginning. And even if you have 50 followers, it doesn't mean that they read everything you write all the time. The best way to get more people to read your tweets is to use hashtags, keywords tagged with #.

In the United States, educators participate in #edchat on Tuesdays, and in the United Kingdom, they have #ukedchat. Teachers vote on a subject they want to discuss, and the theme selected for discussion is announced using a hashtag, such as #edchat. Anyone who uses it will automatically participate in the debate. You can also use hashtags to follow a conference. If you cannot go to a conference, you can still find out what happens by using the conference's hashtag, for example, #Bett20 ★ ★ (London Bett Fair) and #ISTE20 ★ ★ (a yearly conference in the United States).

Whenever you find something interesting, you should consider a "retweet" to send it to those who follow you. It's not the same as answering a post; it's more to say that you think others should read this. You do this by pressing the "*Retweet*" button. When you read an interesting article or blog post, you can share it with others by including a link to the website and who wrote it.

When you start using Twitter, you can choose between Twitter.com, TweetDeck, or Hootsuite, and many other providers, I'm sure. Most are free to use, but Hootsuite is a paid service now, with a free 30-day trial. It's just a matter of taste which one you prefer. Many I know use Twitter as a tool for professional development.

The benefit of using Twitter in professional development is that you can build a network that is not confined to your school or district. When you expand your network beyond geographical boundaries you can connect with teachers who teach the same subjects or student groups as you.

"Online professional development, when carefully tailored to meet local needs and when well integrated with other ongoing technology and professional development plans and initiatives, provides a powerful way for busy educators to meet this challenge successfully" (Power, 2013).

Classroom application

One way to use Twitter is to get in contact with teachers in other countries. I know teachers who use Twitter to get in touch with authors and invite them into the classroom with Skype. Using Twitter is an easy way to get in touch with professionals in many areas. You are not guaranteed a response, but it is exciting to keep up with the discussions you find there. Many people use Twitter when they have questions or when they are looking for good ideas. Many teachers also use Twitter actively with their students. In an educational context, you can use Twitter to keep up with a specific issue, special events, conflicts, elections, or any other news, such as #Brexit, #WorldHealthOrganization. Searching for information? You've probably thought of Google, but why not Twitter? It is easy to be up to date by following newspapers and news channels like BBC and CNN. When you're looking for something special, you can simply search by entering it in your Twitter feed.

Good advice for using Twitter

1. Share quality content. "Fact-check" before you share.
2. Share when those you want to reach are online.
3. Share but not too much.
4. Share new ideas, pedagogy, and exciting lessons.
5. Share with humor, when suitable.
6. Share using appropriate language and proofread everything you share.
7. Share using visual aids such as images or gif files.
8. Share video when it's informative.
9. Share your best messages via your blog (embed) and Facebook.
10. Share Twitter on your blog so people can follow you there.
11. Share by using a hashtag; you reach more people that way.
12. Share by engaging in conversations.
13. Share by tagging those you want to join the conversation.
14. Share by following back those who follow you.
15. Share by creating Twitter lists.

It's also possible to search on Twitter even if you don't have a Twitter account. Maybe you want to try that first? In a search engine, such as Google, enter "Twitter" and what you're looking for.

TWITTER DICTIONARY

Direct message = /DM – when you want only the recipient to see your message
Hashtag = **subject** – messages labeled with #
Favorite = You can click the "star" icon next to any tweet to indicate that it is one of your favorites, for easy reference later
Follow = subscribing to someone's Twitter messages, that is, reading what they write
Followers = people on Twitter who follow you and see your updates on their homepage. Even if you are following someone, it doesn't necessarily mean they will follow you back.
Follow Friday/FF = #FF or #Followfriday is a hashtag used with @mentions to suggest interesting people to their followers.
Replies = using @ sign in the beginning of a tweet to reply to someone. .

Mentions = if you want to include someone in the conversation. Use @ and a person's Twitter name.
Listed/Lists = used for creating lists and adding people on Twitter to group them into categories
Twitterfeed = **Overview** – continuous collection of messages of those you follow
Twittername = a message addressed directly to one or more people that always starts with @, like @annmic. This can appear anywhere in the message.
Retweet = share someone's Twitter message
View conversation = **thread/tweet** – sometimes, you see a message that is clearly part of a conversation/discussion. You can then tap "*View conversation*" and see what has been said/written previously.
URL Shortener = use when you want to include website addresses in your tweet. Bit.ly is a good one to use.

Blogging to publish

A blog is a website where you can publish text and images. A blog is an excellent tool for sharing lesson plans and information with other educators. You can also use the blog with your students. The newest posts are at the top; everything you publish is easy to find and available at any time. I have chosen to use WordPress for my blog. WordPress has a lot of functionalities, and I think it's a good option. I would also recommend edublogs. An edublog is a blog created for educational purposes.

Figure 3.1 is the headline of my blog, "Connected Teaching and Learning," where I share lesson plans and articles on digital teaching and learning. As you can see, I have a Lesson Plans tab, which, in turn, is divided into lesson plans Vg1, lesson plans Vg2, and lesson plans Vg3. In Norway, students attend high school for three years. Many of the lesson plans I share can be used in different subjects and for different age groups. I encourage you to take a look. I have also included other categories: Assessment, The use of technology in school, and professional development.

When I started my blog in 2008, I had very few readers. Slowly the numbers picked up. I think the reason teachers subscribe to the blog is that they find useful lesson plans there and articles about teaching with technology (see Figure 3.2). Using a blog is a good way to share lesson plans and insight on new tools you have discovered. You can also share your articles on Twitter. That way, you might get more readers. You can also read other peoples' blogs and share what you find on your blog. Sometimes you'll find great videos, such as on the TED Talks site. You can post those on your blog; just remember to mention where you found it and who the author of the material is.

ClustrMap (see Figure 3.3) is a visual map service you can use on your blog. It is what we call a widget and a real-time map of your visitors from around the world!

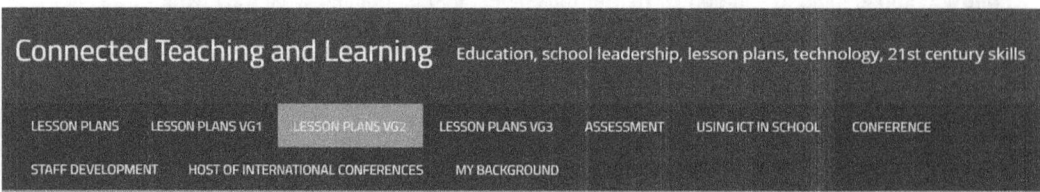

FIGURE 3.1 Headline from my blog

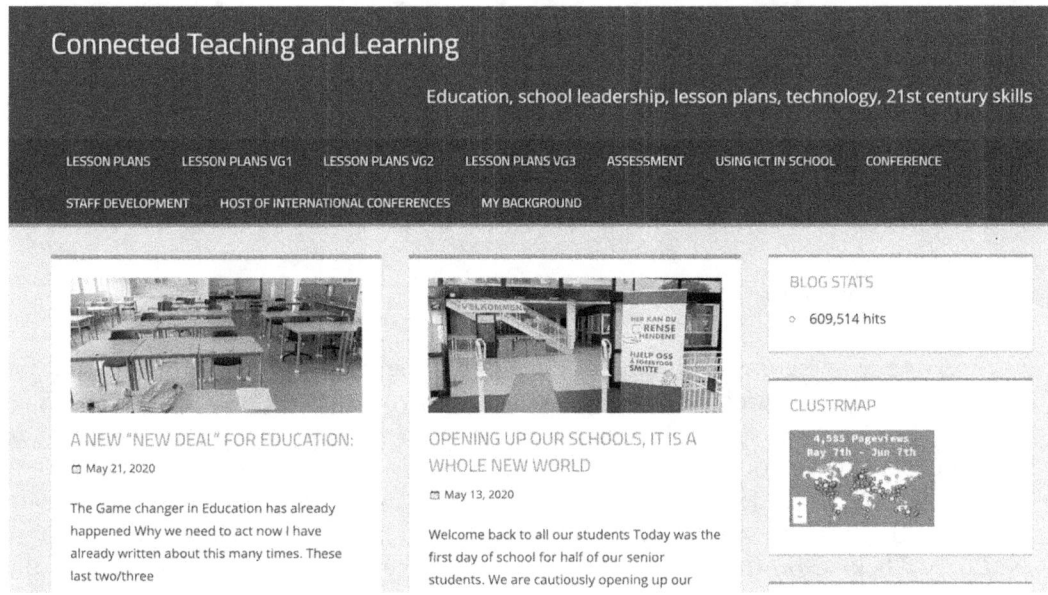

FIGURE 3.2 An example of articles on my blog.

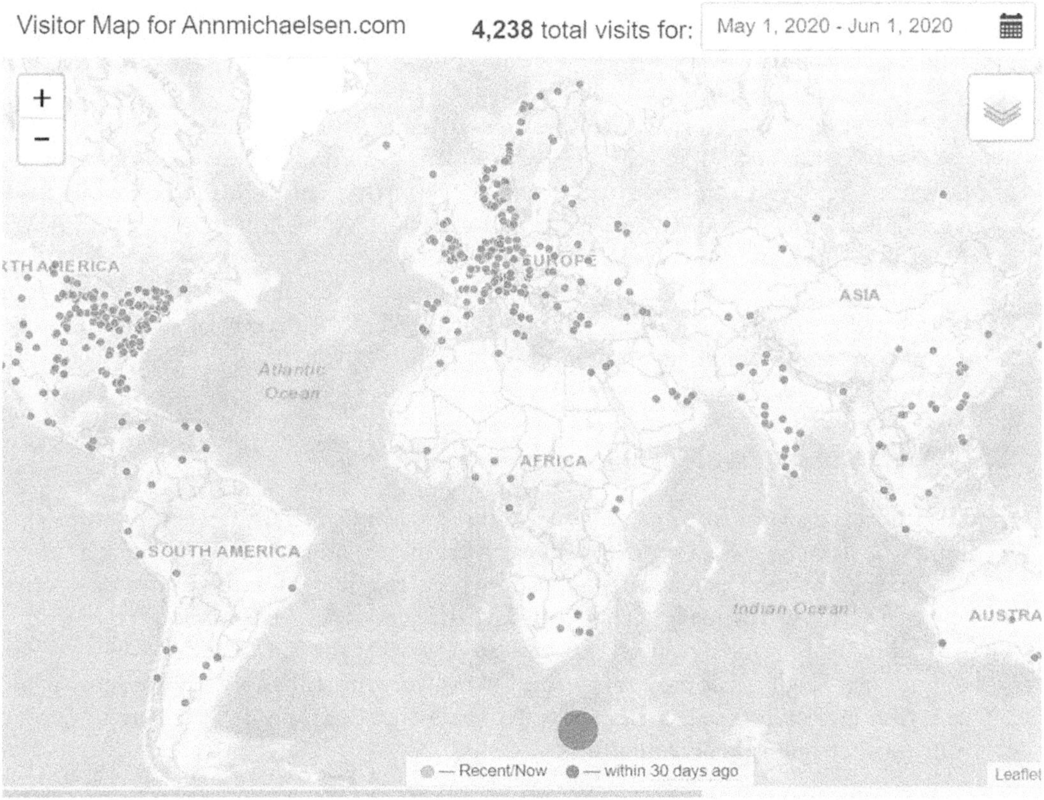

FIGURE 3.3 Map of the world with number of visitors.

FIGURE 3.4 Clustermaps, number of pageviews.

Every time someone clicks on your blog, it is registered. It is very motivating for both teachers and students to see the origin of their readers. ClustrMaps provides an excellent way to see a list of recent visitors to your website. The data you get include the person's exact location.

The larger the dots, the more visitors you have from that city or country. In Figure 3.4, you can see the number of visits to my blog between 5 May and 15 June 2020. Clicking on the map in the browser, you get a more detailed picture of the traffic on the blog.

Classroom application

A blog is an excellent way for students to write and publish their work. And if you want your students to use blogs, you should probably do so as well. It is useful when the teacher sets an example for the students.

Writing a blog is a great way to share lesson plans. Once you have published a post on your blog, it is accessible year after year, and you can find specific material by using the search field. You can search up posts you've written and pin them to your front page. Then it is easy for your students and your readers to find them. In WordPress, you will find this option under "*Visibility Public*."

Working like this is an excellent way to connect with other teachers, especially if they take the time to give you feedback. I often search for material that I published several years ago and update and repost.

RSS, an overview of webpages

RSS collects updates from pages you are interested in on the Internet, continuously and automatically. RSS stands for "Really Simple Syndication" and updates information, such as blog entries, news headlines, or episodes of audio and video series. You don't have to manually check your favorite webpages, because you'll be notified with a link to the updates. It takes some time to set it up, but once it's done, it's easy to use. I use Feedly; it is easy to use, and it was recommended by my students when we wrote the book *Connected Learners* (Michaelsen, 2013). There are many to choose from another one is Feedreader.

Classroom application

An RSS feed will help you to keep track of all the sites you are interested in, such as other teachers' blogs or online newspapers. I use it to keep up with my network of educators and experts in the field. See Figure 3.5. When reading articles online, look for the RSS symbol, perhaps with the additional text "*Sign up for RSS.*" By clicking on the logo, you can subscribe using your RSS feed. Feedly is an RSS reader that is easy to use. RSS is a handy tool to keep track of students' blogs. If your students write blogs, you have to make sure that you read them regularly. RSS will make it easy to see when they have posted a new article. No more searching around; you get everything in the same place.

Create a folder where you collect all your students' blogs, one folder per class. It takes some time to register all the students' blogs, but once it's done, the software is easy to use.

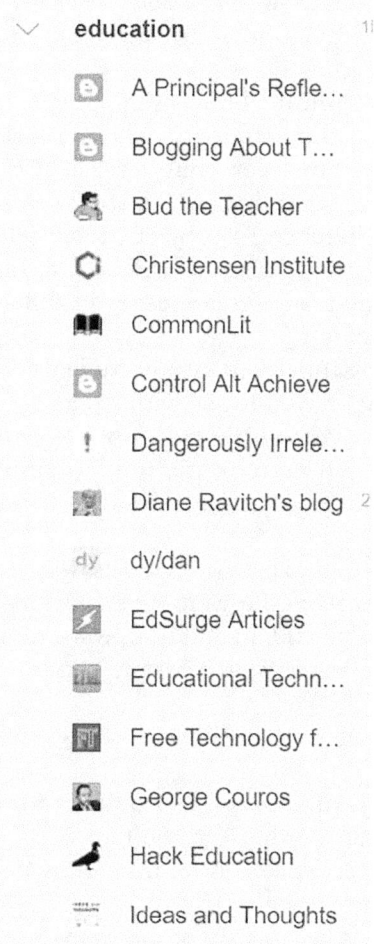

FIGURE 3.5 My RSS feed on education, using Feedly.

Skype, meeting online

Skype is software you can use to reach people around the world. You can use it to make free video calls, have one-to-one and group calls, send instant messages, and share files. Skype is a great way to connect with people you might not otherwise be able to meet. Many teachers already have a Skype account but do not think about using it for networking or professional development. With improved bandwidth in most schools, you will find the quality is excellent. Use your computer connected to a projector and speakers, and just like that, you can invite the whole world into your classroom. The primary takeaway here is that you can get input related to the curriculum goals you are working on with your class. It can be used when discussing different viewpoints, and of course, in language learning. In Norway, one curriculum goal in foreign language learning is "Using communication technology to collaborate and create a meeting with authentic language." A Skype conversation with a class in Europe is an excellent way to do this. There are many subjects, such as history, social science, and religion, to mention some, that conversations with students in other countries can add value to.

Many people are skeptical about using Skype in foreign language learning because they worry that their students' skills are moderate and that the challenge may seem too daunting. However, consider that it can be exciting for students to help others learn their mother tongue! All students, not just Norwegians, can benefit significantly from discussing a subject matter with peers from other places in the world, even if the language is not perfect. Of course, you can also Skype with students who are learning foreign languages in different countries and are on the same level as your students.

Skype has been an essential part of my students' learning this past year, and we have had many exciting conversations with students in China and South Africa. We had a conversation with Peace One Day founder Jeremy Gilley. He spent 40 minutes with my students, and he took the time to answer questions they had on the topic. The time spent on research was rewarded. It was indeed an exciting learning opportunity.

There are many ways to find teachers who use Skype. You can try Twitter, Facebook, or educators who write blogs. How about educators you met on school visits and friends who are teachers abroad. In addition, you can search using Skype in the classroom, a website where you can search for projects for collaboration worldwide.

Classroom application

One thing to consider is time zones. It is difficult for a class in the United States to Skype with students from Europe. On the East Coast of the United States, the time difference compared to Norway is 6 hours, and in California, it is 9 hours. The day is over in Norway before it begins in San Francisco. I have managed to Skype with schools on the East Coast because the students there were willing to come in early.

In elementary school, there are many ways to use Skype. I have a colleague in South Africa who had an exciting project about saving rhinos from extinction. Teachers could sign up on a website and get a stuffed rhino on a visit for a week. During that week, they talked about endangered animal species and completed the project. Skyping with a class was also involved in the project.

If you're looking for projects and partners, you can use "Skype in the Classroom." You can access it using your Skype user name. It's easy to find partners. The tricky part is freeing up time. The project has to be related to the curriculum goals and add to the learning, making it both exciting and relevant. Take time to browse through the different projects with your students. If you do not find anything exciting, you can create your own!

Among younger learners, Mystery Skype is popular. To participate, two teachers agree to a Skype meeting with their students. One class should ask yes-and-no questions only, to find out where in the world the others are. It is always exciting for younger students. If you don't have any contacts, you can go to the Mystery Skype webpage and select "*Find Mystery Skype class now.*" Mystery Skype is a website in the Skype in the Classroom group. You can also search for partners using Twitter; just be sure to search with the hashtag #mysteryskype.

Facebook for networking

Many people are cautious about using Facebook because they are worried that it will take a lot of their time or reluctant to share private matters online. Some who used to be very active on Facebook, are starting to be more restrictive of what they share. It is smart to think about how much time you want to spend on social media. You should know that you can establish and join groups, without having to be friends with the participants. You can also create a secret group with your class, one only you and your students can see. Many schools have groups for teachers and staff. It's a way to keep up to date and share events and informal information. Facebook is also a way to connect with friends around the world – in other words, a smart place to network.

Most likely, all your students are on Facebook, although that might change. It seems like Snapchat and Instagram are more popular these days. My class had a Facebook group where students helped each other with homework and answered questions about school. Another way to use Facebook is to have groups for teachers of specific subjects. If you are lucky, you can get a lot of help and new ideas. One example of a group like this is "English teachers in Norway," where teachers share lesson plans and practical advice.

Facebook is useful for staying up to date because so far, a lot of people use Facebook. Many educators have created groups with different topics, sharing knowledge about pedagogy, technology, and content. There are also separate groups for school leaders.

Keep in mind that you should never write anything on Facebook that you don't want everyone to know, even in closed groups. Apply the network rules that you find in Chapter 8; they are the same for teachers and students. If you decide to use Facebook with your students, make sure that everyone in the class is invited in.

In the Facebook group, students can share documents and notes and help each other, especially on the day before a test. Facebook is also a smart place to conduct a survey. Use the "*Ask a question*" button on the toolbar.

Classroom application

Written by Terje Pedersen, a teacher at Rothaugen Middle School in Bergen, Norway

For the last 6 years, my students and I have used technology and cross-border communication to meet experts and time witnesses on topics we have been reviewing in the classroom. By using digital tools, like closed Facebook groups, Skype, and Google Meet, I have invited people who can add stories to the topics we work on in class. These tools are also used when we contact schools all over the world, discussing various issues. The students say that working with historical topics on a personal level have increased their engagement and connection to the curriculum.

When discussing historical and current conflicts around the world, my students were able to discuss these events with time witnesses. They have discussed the Cold War with a U.S. submarine captain responsible for an atomic submarine in the 1970s and the Vietnam War with a veteran. When studying the Northern Ireland conflict, we talked with an older lady who participated in the demonstrations that occurred during the Bloody Sunday massacre. Students heard the story from those who had participated. This was helpful in their learning because it is easier to understand and comprehend and remember when you hear about it from eyewitnesses.

We have also used Facebook groups with schools from other parts of the world. When students worked on the Cold War theme, they discussed important events with an American middle school class. My students were asked to see the events through the eyes of a communist, while the Americans took the capitalist viewpoint. That was followed by heated discussions on whether the Berlin Wall was the right decision.

One of the most rewarding projects I have done was with a group of students at a juvenile detention center in the United States. After establishing contact with a teacher who worked there, we had the opportunity to ask his students questions about life inside and how they looked at the future. This project was conducted in its entirety on Padlet. My students wrote their questions there, and I sent the link to the teacher. He took the questions to his students, and they responded on pen and paper, and their teacher wrote the answers on our Padlet. Several of the American students chose to respond by writing poems, which made a great impression on my students. After discussing the answers, we compared the differences between the incarceration systems in our two countries. After that, my students chose to illustrate the poems written by the Americans. This project has later been further developed by using Zoom meetings with the administration of the juvenile justice system in South Dakota, where my students first read about the system and then asked questions. Later, when the juvenile detention center was under lockdown due to the COVID-19 situation, we were invited to send Care-Mail. We got connected to an institution in Miami where we sent all our letters, and got replies. We did Zoom meetings with several of the students inside this facility and engaged in a discussion about daily life during COVID-19. The project even got a mention in the *Washington Post*:

> Domenici's nonprofit runs schools at the juvenile detention center and adult jail in New Orleans and provides support to dozens of other schools in youth facilities throughout the country. Word of his Care-Mail program spread quickly

after he wrote about it on Facebook. Soon he had a strikingly varied cadre of volunteers, including a farmer in Virginia, a law professor in Hawaii and a neuroscientist in California. Others include several students based in Norway, Spain and Rwanda as well as Frank Cobarrubia, the podiatrist in Bend, who signed up with his two children, Pilar and Diego.

(Ellison, 2020)

We have also discussed the media's take on the news. An example of this is when we worked on the theme "Girls in India." We read news articles and watched documentaries about how dangerous it is for young girls in India. But we were uncertain about whether this was something that applied to all girls in India. We got in touch with an all-girl school in India and invited them to work with us on this question. They were given access to the same articles that we had read since they were in English. Their teacher discussed this with the class, and the students wrote letters to my students wherein they offered their opinion about the content of the articles. When we later discussed what the Indian students had written, we decided that the picture we had of India was not accurate. Even if there are places in India where girls are in danger, this is not the norm. This gave us an insight into the importance of having reliable sources.

When working on World War I, the students were asked to write journals based on a person who participated in the war. I used my network of experts on the topic. By explaining the project to a Facebook group for World War I experts, I received a lot of useful input with the names of people I could contact. I also came into contact with several family members of soldiers who had participated in World War I and who would be more than happy to contribute. Here, too, we worked with an American class. The students were all assigned fictitious people sending letters back and forth. All this took part in an online book we shared. We finished the project with a Madam Tussaud exhibition where students were characters from the war. They told their story and showed the pictures and drawings they had made.

I have learned a lot through my network on social media. It is easy to get ideas from other teachers who teach the same subject as me. Also, Twitter and Facebook have connected me with many experts in different fields. Some I have even invited to my school. When we studied the Ferguson riots in the United States in the fall of 2014, I connected with Chad Dion Lassiter, a professor of racial politics at the University of Pennsylvania in Philadelphia. He answered my students' questions related to the riots, and my students were able to understand more deeply how complicated issues like these are. In the spring of 2015, we invited Chad Lassiter to our school, and he spent a whole week discussing segregation, Black Lives Matter, and the civil rights struggle in the United States. This visit would never have happened without student participation online.

You might think this is time-consuming, and I have to admit you need to work with colleagues who are willing to help and contribute. I have been so lucky that I have been working with two incredibly skilled teachers at my school. We enjoyed many discussions both about suitable tools to use and how to organize the projects. Most of the tools I use are easy and free to use. I suggest you publish your work with your students using Apple Books, Lulu, or Amazon Kindle, that way you get a wider audience. Fun for the students and fun for you!

An online collaboration between schools in different parts of the world

Norway Lesotho – connecting future leaders

Written by Moliehi Sekese, Mamoeketsi Primary, Lesotho

Being an educator in Africa comes with its challenges as well as opportunities. I personally had a very strong desire to be at the forefront of integrating technology in the classroom. This dream, however, seemed far-fetched considering the fact I was barely computer literate while my school Mamoeketsi Primary Lesotho neither had electricity nor a single computer. These challenges, notwithstanding an opportunity to participate in Microsoft Partners in Learning Education Network, presented itself to me in 2009. I was thrilled when I won the National and Continental titles of this prestigious initiative. This culminated in an international forum, where I met Ann, who was a participant from Sandvika High School in Norway. We clicked instantly, and it became apparent that we shared the same passion for technology integration in education. We, therefore, came up with an online collaboration between our schools.

As a way of keeping in touch with one another, we started communicating through Facebook, Skype, and blogs. We periodically engaged our learners in Skype sessions, where they shared information among themselves. Some of the lessons that our students participated in were "What is life like in their respective countries" and "Things that are common and different in both countries." These peer-learning exercises have improved my learners' knowledge and communicating skills as they were no longer shy to share information with their international counterparts.

I further introduced my learners to the creation of blogs where they first started by commenting on Ann and her students' blogs on issues that show the importance of technology. After creating their blogs, they expressed their educational aspirations. Their counterparts excitedly commented on their blogs. Our efforts to integrate technology in teaching and learning have yielded the good fruits again. They brought about the exchange program between Ann's students and my learners, whereby her students would visit my learners and help them with advanced computer skills that enhanced their online learning.

As a way of improving our network, Ann and her students saw a need to help my school with the establishment of a well-furnished computer laboratory and internet connectivity. This development has created a better learning experience for my learners since they are able to Skype with their counterparts more often. The availability of the new computer laboratory not only helps my learners, but it also helped our neighboring schools where they would gather in our computer lab to do coding during the Africa Code Week.

Meeting Ann epitomizes the vision I always have of exposing my learners to the global world. Technology allows us to collaborate and combine our knowledge and expertise.

Act2connect us – a student-driven collaboration

Written by a former student at Sandvika high school, Tobias Langås Handeland

If you a November morning would find yourself in the main streets of any Norwegian city, there is a chance that some Norwegian teenagers would offer you some cake and coffee for a charity project. Every autumn, students from all across the country wake up early to bake cakes, make coffee, clean offices, or work a day for an organization. The students do this in solidarity with people who do not have the same opportunities as themselves. What they earn from their work often goes to support children's right to education and strengthen the rights of those who have few or almost no rights at all. A vast majority of Norwegian high schools support a charity organization that runs many projects all around the world. Sandvika High School, however, has been unique. Students and teachers at Sandvika chose to support Mamoeketsi primary school in Maseru, Lesotho. The project is called "Act2connect.us" and takes place one day every year when students work to support Mammoeketsi.

The Lesotho project's focus on one single school has been the key to its success. Through excellent and direct communication and almost zero administration costs, the progress has been quick and overwhelming. Thanks to the excellent cooperation between Mammoeketsi and Sandvika, hundreds of students have received scholarships and are now able to attend high school. Furthermore, the unique partnership between the schools made teacher and student exchanges possible. Students and teachers from Sandvika and Maseru have visited each other frequently. It is a unique opportunity for sharing and dialogue.

Over the past years, the project has helped create an understanding of different cultures. In particular, students at Sandvika have had their worldviews and their perceptions of everyday life in Lesotho challenged. Many did not know anything about the country, but Act2connect.us has given us a far more diverse and reality-based view of Lesotho compared to what one often receives from the media. In addition, the project has improved many children's education and, for some, made dreams come true. Teenagers from Sandvika want to work hard because they see that their efforts matter and that it leads to rapid change for the better. Finally, because of the exchange of students and teachers, a unique friendship developed between the two schools. A friendship where one can exchange ideas and support each other. The importance of this project will continue to grow in the globalized world we live in.

Reaching out to a wider audience

Students tell their story to BBC World Service

Written by Lisa Gabrielsen, Sandvika High School, Sandvika, Norway

While schools in Norway were closed due to the coronavirus pandemic, I met my English class students in weekly video meetings on Teams. I knew that some students were finding it very hard to be away from school and their friends, and they spent a lot of time sitting in their rooms (and often in their beds, our Teams meetings revealed). I happened to hear on the radio that BBC World Service/Response invited people from around the world to record their experiences of how life had changed during this time of (more or less) global lockdown (BBC World News Service, 2020).

My students got the following task: Film your story for the global radio station BBC World Service and answer the following question: How has the corona pandemic affected you as a student in Norway? Go outside and film your corona story (up to 5 minutes) on your phone. Email your film to BBC World Service and share pictures and comments on our shared Padlet.

My students responded very well to this task. Some took their neighbor's dog out for a walk, and others went down to the empty football stadium and explained how all sports had been put on hold. Several students made excellent informative films describing our school system and how this lockdown in Norway changed how we celebrated our national day. As their teacher, I was impressed with how they took ownership of this task. I was also profoundly moved by how honest they were about how this lockdown was affecting them. They understood their global audience and represented Norwegian teenagers and students in an excellent way. Although they went for walks on their own, they shared their experience on Padlet and commented on each other's photos with humor and friendliness. It turned out to be not an individual task but a group experience.

You can imagine the excitement when I received an email from a journalist at the BBC World Service a week later asking if they could use a couple of the recordings in one of the Response programs on the radio. For my students to be able to reach a global audience was a unique experience. Their voices would be heard!

References

BBC World News Service. (2020, June 4). *Share your story about the coronavirus.* From The Response: https://www.bbc.co.uk/programmes/articles/16DGBv0FxxwRHXlk392HSpR/share-your-story-about-the-coronavirus-outbreak

Ellison, K. (2020, May 26). *Care-Mail delivers pandemic pen pals to juveniles in lockdown.* From the Washington Post: https://www.washingtonpost.com/local/public-safety/care-mail-delivers-pandemic-pen-pals-to-juveniles-in-lockdown/2020/05/23/9f0284a4-9b67-11ea-ad09-8da7ec214672_story.html

Michaelsen, A. S. (2013). *Connected learners: A step-by-guide to creating a global classroom.* Virgiania Beach, VA: Powerful Learning Practice Press.

Power, K.-A. K. (2013). *Professional learning on Twitter: A content analysis of professional learning conversations among self-organized groups of educators.* From Scholarship at UWindsor: https://scholar.uwindsor.ca/cgi/viewcontent.cgi?article=5899&context=etd

CHAPTER 4

Tablet PCs in primary and middle school

Simen Spurkland

Introduction

Even if many schools buy tablet PCs for their students, teachers are still struggling to find a good pedagogical use of them. This chapter shows you how tablets PCs can enhance learning and what it does to your teaching. I'm a middle school teacher, and I had my first experience with tablet PCs in 2011 when my school bought eight iPads. Two years later, I became part of an expert group in 1:1 coverage of iPads in schools. Since then, all my students have had iPads, and I have had ample opportunity to explore and create functional and sustainable teaching and learning environments for my students. Since 2011, I have participated in countless workshops over the years as both a participant and a speaker.

In this chapter, I share my experiences with using tablets in middle school. The content is transferable to both higher and lower grades. The examples I share here coincide with the rest of the book. I show examples from the following subjects: music, social science, and mathematics. I also include information on general use. You can use any tablet PC, but I use examples from the iPad because it is my opinion that it works well and because my expertise is in using it.

Apps for music lessons

Music is a subject I have taught since I graduated from teachers college in 2000. It is a hands-on subject, which is often an advantage because students regard practical classes as a useful variation from the more academic subjects. But the same practicality presents challenges precisely because younger students are still working on motor skills and coordination. Few students have any experience in playing musical instruments, and chords on a guitar can be difficult for small hands and short fingers. I meet my students for 60 minutes every week. Seventy-five percent of the time, there are two teachers, and our groups consist of 15 students each. To teach 15 students how to play the guitar is a challenge, to say the least, but using a tablet PC makes it a lot easier.

First, the distribution of songs, chords, instructions, and tasks is effortless. If a student wants to play a new song, it only takes me a few minutes to make the song with the right chords available to the student.

When the student wants to work on rhythm, several apps offer ways for the student to practice accompaniment. Interaction and rhythm alone are two of the most demanding elements of making music.

When a student asks for help with grip or rhythm, I show them the same way I have always done. But now the student can record this specific instruction and save it to their iPad. The same occurs when the student receives ongoing summative assessment: the conversation can be recorded, and the student can revisit the recording anytime. That way, they know what needs to be improved. An essential element of learning is to see progress. It is not always enough to just look at the end product, both because the distance from the starting point is not clear and because many factors influence the immediate outcome. It's incredible how scary the students think it is when they know I will be evaluating their product in the end. To make it easier for them, I have my students deliver a short video log at the end of each lesson. In about 30 seconds, they show me where they are in the process. With five such short logs, I can, at the end of the process, go in and look at how the student has improved from week to week.

In addition to this, the GarageBand (GB) app has added to the quality of my teaching. I would like to add that this app is only available for IPad. In short, GB turns your iPad and iPhone into a collection of touch instruments and a full-featured recording studio – so you can make music anywhere you go. And with live loops, it makes it easy for anyone to have fun creating music like a DJ. You can use multi-touch gestures to play keyboards and guitars, and create beats that make you sound like a pro – even if you've never played a note before (Apple, 2020).

GB makes it easy to create seemingly advanced music. If you break the code, you'll have an entire band available in no time, or you might sound like Kygo almost by accident. Even if students can make music that instantly sounds good, it is not difficult to detect if it is superficial. It doesn't help them to sound professional when they start if what they do becomes repetitive or monotonous. After using GB, I knew that the way we had worked with music composing earlier did not have the learning outcome I had hoped for. My students have always managed to get to a certain level in practical guitar or piano playing, whereby they learn how a song is built and manage to keep a rhythm for a long time. But when I started using GB, I was surprised by how little understanding of music students had – even though for several weeks they had played through a 12-bar blues on guitar. Their competence in playing the instrument did not reflect a deeper understanding of music as I initially had thought it had.

The challenge is finding ways to combine different musical competencies in various products and formats. It has given me great moments of advanced compositions but also some troubling revelations that it is hard to evaluate their end product.

It is a challenge to get students up to a level where they become genuinely creative. Often, the processes stop in the absence of mastery of purely practical elements, such as placing fingers on the keys or sore fingertips after much practice on the guitar. These are the challenges that I indeed still work on and want to get students to master but now, luckily, in combination with the opportunities that the tablet PCs offer. The tasks that can be given and solved digitally provide students with ways to express themselves and allow them to be creative without being constrained by the lack of mastery of playing an instrument. When successful, it gives a self-reinforcing effect, finding their creativity on the iPad makes students want to re-create the experience on an instrument.

My experience is that I can help my students in their musical development on a very different level than when using instruments in class.

Classroom application

In all subjects, good examples are essential and necessary and serve as something students can model and re-create. This is particularly important when using tablet PCs in music. If you show your student how a creative task can be solved, a clear majority of students will be able to do this. Therefore, it is crucial to choose good examples so that students understand the required level. By modeling others, they build competency to become creative and go from there to the stage of improvisation. You need to have a high level of skills in music to be able to improvise.

It is also a good idea to be aware of the use of video as a resource for learning. Every time my students start figuring out which song they want to play on either guitar or piano, the vast majority of them are drawn to YouTube's universe of instructional movies. My advice is to be cautious about that because they might prove too complicated for the majority of students.

Online resources in social science classes

In middle school in Norway, the same teacher usually works with history, geography, and social science. Typically, we will deal with conflicts, natural disasters, how the world has evolved, politics, and interpersonal relations. Dates and years, names of sea and mountains, historical figures, and other facts are still important – but they are easily accessible. Put simply, one can say that if the answer to the question can be Googled, then the question is not good enough. We need to work with building students' knowledge and skills and developing their critical thinking and reflection. When all students have tablet PCs, we need to change our teaching.

An example of how digital devices enrich teaching is the use of videos like *The Fallen of World War II*. Here, you can see the number of fallen in various conflicts throughout world history. The precise figure of fatal casualties in a battle shows the cruelty of a conflict. Just looking at the numbers in a book does not have the same effect. Resources like these make them more understandable.

I use Google Maps to zoom in and out on different places in the world. When it is time to look at the world from another perspective, for instance, population growth and poverty, I use Gapminder (see Figure 4.1). Gapminder is an independent Swedish foundation with no political, religious, or economic affiliations. Gapminder is a fact tank, not a think tank. Gapminder produces free teaching resources to help students understand the world based on reliable statistics. Gapminder promotes a fact-based worldview everyone can understand. Gapminder is a website with visualizing tools that show how people live, with examples from almost all over the world (see Figure 4.2). This type of insight makes it easier to understand the differences and to challenge students' general perceptions and prejudices. Using a large amount of data

FIGURE 4.1 Categories to search for using Gapminder.

FIGURE 4.2 Illustration of questions answered in Gapminder.

presented visually based on facts, you can give social science teaching an extra dimension (Gapminder, 2020).

The most significant change I have made in the social sciences class is to make sure that my students produce multimedia or multimodal texts. One example is when the students study World War II. The end product has to include an extensive reflective text, a detailed source list, and a video in which they reflect on how they have worked with the material and sources and how they reached their conclusion. I quickly found out that it was difficult to establish if the work was authentic. A lot of the material is online. What I did as a solution was to have students give me a log of their work in the form of a video. When I looked at the videos, I immediately knew their work was authentic and how they had reached their conclusions.

Some students used the video to read the text they had delivered, without empathy, without looking at the camera, without showing any signs that they knew the material. Other students again spoke directly to the camera, did not have scripts, reflected on the process, and showed a credible commitment to what they had produced. They were able to share challenges and how they had worked through that. I stopped looking to see if the students had plagiarized and concentrated on understanding the connection between text and video. It allowed me to spend more time looking for qualities in the product rather than suspecting that it was not the student's work. This experience is an excellent example of how the teacher can concentrate on helping students create products with a combination of image/sound and text/presentations. It makes the assessment more relevant and more vibrant, and students will have to invest more in the products to get to the finish line. Such a change in the requirements of the products means that students can show the depth of their competence.

Classroom application

In these subjects, students must have "voice and choice" to lay the foundation for more in-depth learning. What we need to remember is that the tasks should be relevant to the students, and the teacher has to provide sufficient time combined with enough freedom/control to the student. When you give the student choice, you do not in detail decide what the end product should look like but help define which direction the product should take. You want to move from a teacher-led classroom to an environment where the student takes charge. The student has to ask the questions. For example, how do you win a war? Students usually know when a war starts and ends and who fought against whom, but it is more challenging to explain the outcome. Show the students how to ask interesting questions and throw yourself into the academic conversations that occur among students – that is where the learning takes place.

Apps and video in math

The use of digital tools, such as spreadsheets and dynamic graphs, has been included in the exams in Norway for several years now. Unless every student has a device, it is challenging to teach this way.

Spreadsheets, or Numbers, as the app is called on iPad, is well suited for documenting data that later can be interpreted and presented. It can be anything from simple surveys to the documentation of measurements. "Numbers is the most innovative spreadsheet app ever designed for a mobile device. Created exclusively for iPad, iPhone, and iPod touch, Numbers includes support for Multi-Touch gestures and Smart Zoom so you can create powerful spreadsheets using just your fingers" (Apple, 2020).

I start work with spreadsheets this way: my students produce five different paper planes that they throw ten times each before measuring length, floating time, and variation in altitude. Most students know terms like *average* and *median*, but visualizing it this way gives them a deeper understanding of the concepts. When they can find the numbers based on their measurements and assess whether it is the average or the median that explains the overall characteristics of the aircraft, the chances of a real understanding is higher.

GeoGebra is dynamic mathematics software for all levels of education that brings together geometry, algebra, spreadsheets, graphing, statistics, and calculus in one easy-to-use package (see Figure 4.3). GeoGebra is a rapidly expanding community of millions of users located in just about every country. GeoGebra has become the leading provider of dynamic mathematics software, supporting science, technology, engineering, and mathematics education and innovations in teaching and learning worldwide (GeoGebra, 2020).

I start with a fun task just to introduce this tool to my students. Students draw a self-portrait using various geometric shapes. The goal is to begin by building familiarity with the software. After working with the tools over time, my students were more confident in their usage as the time for the exam approached. I have to add that GeoGebra is a very advanced tool for students to use in mathematics. I recommend that teachers explore the functions they offer.

I use videos a lot in math. Short videos based on what we have been working on in the previous lesson help students catch up. With 30 students, it is a known fact that

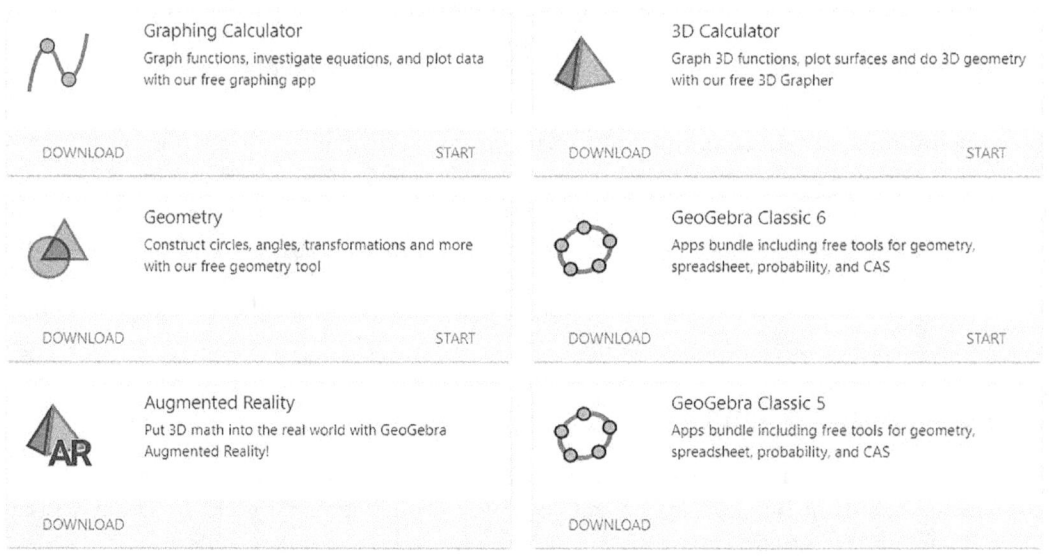

FIGURE 4.3 The different functions found in GeoGebra.

many do not get it the first time. If you make a video, you can explain concepts that need repetition. I often make videos summarizing the assignments for my students (see Chapter 6 for more on the flipped classroom).

Reversing the roles here is also a good idea. Have your students make a video to explain mathematical concepts. Sometimes students come up with the right solutions without showing how they arrived at the result. Teaching this in a video is a good way for students to show their competencies (Sfard, 2015). Anna Sfard (2019) calls this commognition, a word composed of *communication* and *cognition*:

> Commognition
> Exploring the relationship between thinking and communication has led Professor Sfard to develop the theory of commognition. This blend of communication and cognition defines a theory that regards thinking as a form of internal communication. This communication is multimodal, almost never in words only. Sometimes, it is entirely non-verbal. Sfard developed the notion of commognition within the context of mathematics education as a response to weaknesses she observed in the traditional views of human development.
>
> Anna Sfard (2019)

Using video, in this case, gives me the opportunity to assess the process. In some cases, this may be the only way some students get to express themselves. Shy students might not participate much in class. Making a video like this helps these students.

Another application I use is Explain Everything for iPad. This app is described in detail in Chapter 6, "The Flipped Classroom."

Changing the way you assess students' work

Assessing student work is always a challenge. My experience is that assessing the process can be just as valuable as assessing the end product. And successful teaching in a digital classroom means moving away from written tests with paper and pencils. I encourage my students to make videos of their work, alone or in groups. iMovie is my choice, but there are a lot of other products out there. The editing capabilities of iMovie allow cutting, adding and editing of audio tracks, and a lot of other elements that quickly make the products look professional. That it looks good helps increase students' motivation and adds to the sense of mastering a difficult subject. It also increases the motivation to work with projects.

> With a streamlined design and intuitive Multi-Touch gestures, iMovie lets you create Hollywood-style trailers and beautiful movies like never before.
> - Choose from 14 trailer templates with stunning graphics and original scores by some of the world's top film composers
> - Customize movie studio logos, cast names, and credits.
> - Select the best videos and photos for your trailer with the help of animated drop zones
> - Record video for your trailer right in iMovie.
>
> (Apple, 2020)

In fact, the video log requirement applies to every subject I teach. During music classes, for example, they make a 30-second video log after each session; an example of that is when they are learning how to play guitar. This provides useful information for the final assessments. It makes for interesting observations to follow my students in the five weeks it takes to master playing the guitar. A final evaluation in a subject in which the students have to perform can often be clouded by students' nerves. This method allows the process to count just as much as the end product. This makes assessment transparent for both students and the teacher.

In social sciences, history, or geography, I use group interviews that the students record themselves. The students draw a topic that they discuss in groups of four. They are assessed on specific, known criteria. They are also encouraged to help fellow group members. Many subjects in Norway require oral tests, and in a class of 30, that is very time-consuming. When they record their conversations, and I can watch and assess them in the comfort of my home or office.

Many teachers teach without the use of textbooks in Norway; this accelerated after we all started using iPads. That said, the transition could prove difficult for many teachers. Relying on a textbook is easy and predictable. Venturing outside that safe zone can be daunting. I think moving away from relying on textbooks is necessary when using tablet PCs in primary and middle school and, as this book points out, in high school as well.

Information flow is easy in a digital classroom. Every important message from the teacher is posted on the learning platform we use. Using a good learning platform is smart when teachers post information in the same places. And students are familiar with where to look for information, assignments, grades, and homework.

I tell my students that the time we spend together in class is what has the most effect on their learning. I want them to feel good about the time spent with me and feel that they have done their best when we part each day. It is important that they document their learning process, just as I discussed earlier. I ask them to leave traces of learning that guide me in my teaching and tell me what was easy and what needs more work. Compared to an analog classroom with notebooks, these logs can give the students and me vital information. I am talking about short video logs, audio tracks, lyrics, poems, pictures, presentations, and movies or screenshots of how far they have come in a game or with a song in GB. It is helpful for teachers to spot students struggling in certain areas as early as possible. The classroom becomes more transparent, and I know more about the students than I did before. It also gives me the opportunity to guide those students who have come shortest in their process, without first having to go through a test or other potentially stressful situations. Working toward graduation, we work on formative assessment, and students can improve their outcome throughout the process.

Some things to consider

As mentioned earlier in this book, good classroom management is very important when all your students have tablet PCs. It is also good to know about all the different apps and software available. Most likely, your school has decided on what they want their teachers to use. There is a jungle of apps and different services out there, and those in charge need to be skilled in this area. Tools and software should have the right qualities and a natural place in the classroom. The focus should always be on the students' learning and helping them toward mastery. Fancy new tools are tempting, but they need to be tested to know that they do the job:

1   The introduction of digital technology in itself is no guarantee of positive change or that learning is taking place. There needs to be a change of pedagogy to align with the new environment. The same pedagogy used in a traditional classroom will not work.

2   The outcome depends on the teacher. How well they can transform the learning from teacher-led to student-centered. In this environment, the student has to be in charge and take control of their education. Remember student voice and choice!

Hopefully, many teachers in your school are either working like this or looking into it. Working together in teams to get an overview of all that is out there is the only way to navigate in this digital world. Don't get stressed if things do not work out as you thought they would. The most experienced teachers often have a plan B and a plan C. Take your time so that you feel comfortable teaching this way. And if you make a mistake, that is okay too. In this environment, we are all learners. That is the fun part!

References

Apple. (2020, June 5). *GarageBand*. From App Store Preview: https://apps.apple.com/us/app/garageband/id408709785

Gapminder. (2020, June 4). *Almost nobody knows the basic global facts!* From Gapminder: https://www.gapminder.org/

GeoGebra. (2020, June 4). *GeoGebra math apps*. From GeoGebra: https://www.geogebra.org/?lang=en

Sfard, A. (2015). *Learning, commognition and mathematics*. London: Sage.

Sfard, A. (2019, June). *Learning, commognition and mathematics*. From Reach Outreach: https://researchoutreach.org/articles/human-learning-story-identity-communication/6

CHAPTER

5

Cooperative learning

Ann S. Michaelsen

Introduction

In the next two chapters, I explain how digital tools can contribute to learning when using cooperative learning and in the flipped classroom. I start with cooperative learning. I first heard about cooperative learning when I attended a workshop in Oslo. My interest in this teaching method led me to Canada, where I participated in a workshop with educators from 33 different Norwegian schools. Cooperative learning dates back to the 1930s when researchers found that people who cooperate and work together to achieve shared goals were more successful in attaining outcomes than those who strived independently to complete the same goals. In 1975, David and Roger Johnson identified that cooperative learning promoted mutual liking, better communication, high acceptance, and support, as well as demonstrated an increase in a variety of thinking strategies among individuals in the group (History of Cooperative Learning, n.d.). I met Roger and David in Oslo in 2004 and attended their workshop. After that, I have strongly supported the use of cooperative learning in the classroom.

What is cooperative learning?

Cooperative learning is dividing the class into small groups of students and helping them with strategies to work together and support each other. Students are divided into small groups for one class period or several weeks to achieve shared learning goals and complete jointly specific tasks and assignments. It is smart to use groups of four because you can alternate between groups of four and pairs when needed.

Cooperative learning builds on five basic elements

1. Equal participation
2. Positive interdependence

3. Individual and group accountability
4. Social skills training
5. Face-to-face promotive interaction

The idea behind cooperative learning is found in the first point: "equal participation." Traditional teamwork can often end with only one or two in the group doing all the work. However, by controlling how the members of the group work, you avoid the unequal division by dividing the tasks evenly between all the participants. The teacher, who knows the students well, groups the students accordingly, making sure that no student gets tasks they cannot master. You may want to number the students from one to four and divide the tasks given based on the ability of the student. When organizing the classroom, set it up so that the students sit face-to-face. The use of computers can be restricted to one per group. The focus should be on the interaction between the students, not what they find on the computer. As always, it is essential that the teacher takes the lead and facilitates computer use. Our teachers organize the classroom before the students enter. Later in this chapter, I provide examples of where digital devices are particularly useful in cooperative learning. The main point is that the teacher is in charge and has a clear vision of how the students learn best. If all four students have a computer, it is more difficult to obtain the desired effect of cooperative learning. It is, however, possible.

Individual accountability applies to all the assessment situations that occur in class. Each student should receive individual feedback. Often, ordinary group work can be unfair when the workload is differently distributed among the students and they all get the same grade.

Cooperative learning is a great way to improve your students' social skills – many of the exercises given in this chapter work well when starting with a new class. The students get to know each other, and the teacher creates a safe environment in the classroom. Exercises in which students get to know each other can include talking about their hobbies, favorite food, or subjects in school, and must be time-managed so that everyone has the same amount of time to talk. We all know how it is to be in a group with people who dominate the conversation. Cooperative base groups are long-term, heterogeneous cooperative learning groups with stable membership. Members' primary responsibilities are to (a) ensure all members are making good academic progress (i.e., positive goal interdependence), (b) hold each other accountable for striving to learn (i.e., individual accountability), and (c) provide each other with support, encouragement, and assistance in completing assignments (i.e., promotive interaction); (Johnson & Johnson, n.d.).

Face-to-face promotive interaction implies that the students help each other by sharing resources and looking out for their teammates. They help, support, encourage, and praise each other's efforts to learn.

The last point revolves around the process of working in teams. Each member must reflect on their own participation as well as the group's. When using cooperative learning, students learn how to work with everyone in the class, not a selective few.

As a school leader, I often visit classrooms to observe teachers and students. I sometimes see that teachers ask questions, and the same students raise their hands and respond. That way, three-quarters of the class know they are off the hook and relax.

Using cooperative learning, you can activate all your students. The students discuss the topics in their group after you ask your question, it gives time for the whole group to respond, and they all get a better understanding of what they are learning.

You can find cooperative learning research dated back to 1920. "The widespread use of cooperative learning is due to multiple factors. Three of the most important are that cooperative learning is clearly based on theory, validated by research, and operationalized into clear procedures educators can use" (Johnson, Johnson, & Stanne, 2000). The competency students build when they work in a cooperative learning environment promotes better learning outcomes than does traditional teaching. I have observed how students are more conscious of their role in the group and how they work on helping everyone contribute equally. I see this in classes where the teachers have been working on student inclusion and teaching students what they need to do to make their teammates perform better. Often students will discover that helping others is just as productive as working alone or even better. One of the goals here is that everyone gets an equal chance to contribute.

However, students are not necessarily active just because they work in groups. How the teacher organizes the group work is vital.

To organize the interactions between students who are working in cooperative learning teams, we use learning structures. Most teachers will typically adopt some favorite structures that they use regularly. Each cooperative learning structure, or strategy, consists of very specific steps.

Next I look at some of the structures that work well with digital tools.

Tasks to create a safe working environment for students

When school starts in the fall, I use these structures to help students get to know the rest of the class and work in an inclusive environment. During the school year, you may want to change groups many times so that everyone has a chance to work together.

Parking lot

The parking lot is often used in cooperative learning. Traditionally, it is a poster the teacher hangs by the door where students can pose questions or concerns when they leave the class. It can be done during a lesson or activity. The teacher can then address those questions at the end of the class or the beginning. I usually do it at the end of the day. I use a Padlet or Talkwall for this particular activity. That way, we can go back in time and see if anything has changed. When I do this, I use the following headlines: "What Is Going Well," "What Are the Questions," "Ideas for Improvement," and "Concerns"; see Figure 5.1. After each subject lesson, you ask your students to comment by providing a link. It is a great way to get feedback both for the teacher and the students. They do this anonymously. That way, they can be honest and not afraid of the teacher's reactions. I find it reassuring that the students see for themselves that one thing they do not like, others do. For example, some would say too much work, too much reading or writing, and then others would say the opposite.

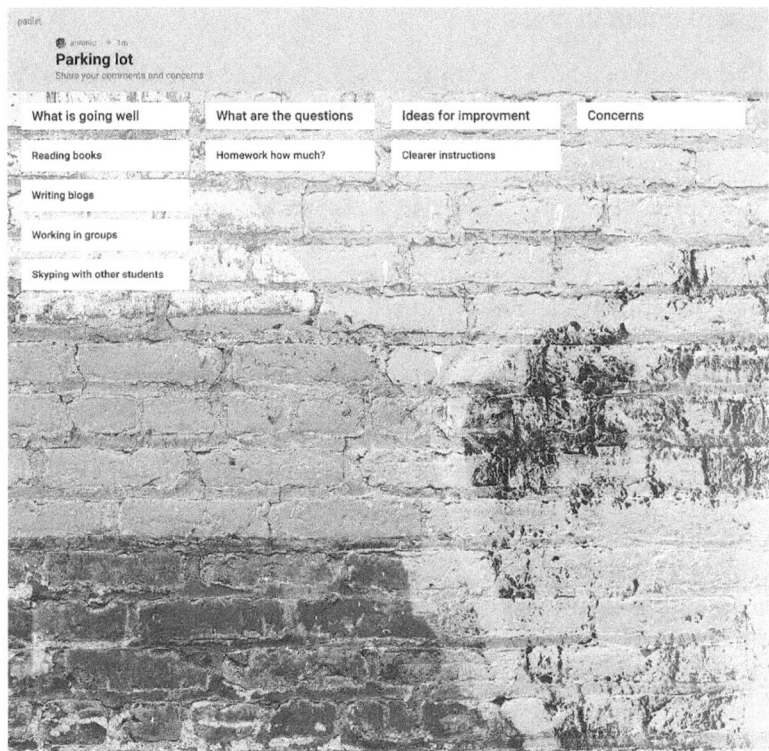

FIGURE 5.1 An example of the parking lot using Padlet.

Think–pair–share

When you ask a question, ask students to first think about the answer without raising their hands. Many students need a little think time. Teachers may be afraid of a silence period, but often a few minutes are all that's needed to offer students time to reflect. Then pair the students. No one gets to raise their hand and answer yet. Instead, they discuss the topic with their shoulder partner. Now it is time to ask students in your class, but this time you ask what the shoulder partner said. That way, you make sure that they have to listen to each other when discussing the topic. Way too often, students don't take time to pay attention to what their classmates say. This also applies when the whole group is working on a problem. Ask for a specific numbered group member if he or she can tell you what the group discussed. That way, everyone has to pay attention. When the group has addressed a topic, it is easier for students who are reluctant to raise their hands and speak in class to participate. Once the group has reached a consensus, you know the students have had time to learn together. Sometimes you can remind them that they cannot move on before the whole group knows the material. Working like this, you can get 100 percent participation, if not, at least double of that in a traditional classroom.

Think–pair–share notes in class

A lot of classroom teaching is with the use of a whiteboard or PowerPoint presentation. Many question the use of lecturing since we tend to see that after 15 to 20 minutes, students at middle and high school level start to think about something else. When we choose to lecture, we have some alternatives.

"Lectures provide a good entry into a topic; they provide context and the level of detail and comprehension that are required for a particular class" (Bradbury, 2016).

I suggest that you break up your lectures, and I explain how to do this here. After 10 minutes, ask students to reflect on what they have heard. If you allow students to take notes, have them look at their notes. Students then share their thoughts and notes with their group. To be sure that everyone has understood the topic, the teacher asks one in each group to explain. If everyone has understood the material, the teacher can continue with the lecture.

Another way to break up a lecture is to use peer instruction:

> The goal of PI [peer instruction] is to transform the lecture environment so that it actively engages students and focuses their attention on underlying concepts. Instead of presenting the level of detail covered in the textbook or lecture notes, lectures consist of several short presentations on key points, each followed by a ConcepTest – short conceptual questions, typically posed in a multiple-choice format, on the subject being discussed.
> (Crouch, Watkins, Fagen, & Mazur, 2007)

Apps to use for this way of working include the following:

Pingo: Use PINGO for checking in on learning goals, creating tag clouds, engaging your class, and collecting anonymous feedback from your students.
Microsoft Teams does the same if you do a survey using polls.

Most learning systems offer this functionality too.

Another way to make sure students get all the essential facts right is to assign some specific students to be notetakers for the class. They can do this by co-writing a document in Google Docs, Word Online, or in a OneNote Class notebook. That way, everyone has all the notes, even if they were absent that day. I think it is a good idea to use a OneNote Class notebook. Each group can have a section, and the teacher can look through the notes and see if there are any misunderstandings or confusing parts. (See Chapter 2 for how to do this.) If you do use lecture as a teaching method, it may be interesting to discuss with your students how they learn best and if they know how to take notes. There have been many discussions if taking notes on a computer has the same effect as using pen and paper. Many researchers have suggested that laptop note-taking is less effective than longhand note-taking for learning. In three studies, we found that students who took notes on laptops performed worse on conceptual questions than students who took notes longhand (Mueller & Oppenheimer, 2014). At our school, we recommend that students buy a PC that has a digital pen for taking notes.

Not all students are good at digital note-taking because they are often distracted. I know many teachers who let some of their students take notes on their computers, while others have to use pen and paper. Some students like to get the presentation from the teacher before class and then listen to the lecture without taking notes. They remember more that way. It is possible to work on this with your students. Let them test how well they do. They might very well improve their skills.

Jigsaw – reading new material

When introducing new and challenging material, you can divide the content into four different sections. Each student in a group will read a different part. After reading, new groups are formed with students who have read the same material, like all number 1s, 2s, and so on. They meet to discuss and clarify what they have read. When the content is understood, they return to their original group to share what they have learned.

Using Kindles and iPads, students can highlight important areas of what they have read and share it with their group. They can also add the text they want to read in OneNote and use the notes feature to highlight. This task works well as group work where each member reads a specific part of the text. In this structure, students practice how to give a clear summary of the material to the rest of the group. Another way the teacher can be sure everyone has understood all the parts is to have the groups create a quiz with Kahoot. The questions they make there will reveal how well they have understood the material. If you have students with dyslexia and the text is in OneNote, they can use the Immersive Reader and have the text read aloud to them. See Chapter 2 for information about OneNote and Chapter 9 for information about the use of Immersive Reader.

Apps for learning new material

There are many apps for memorizing new material. To be used individually or with other students in groups. Memory cards to study for a specific topic, for instance.

Anki can be downloaded to your computer for easy making of flashcards.
Quizlet has many flashcards in different categories that are ready to use. The teacher can make them, or more preferable, the students should make their own.
StudyStack also lets you search for free flashcards shared by students and teachers. It is easy to use.

Collaborate on presentations

An alternative to students presenting in class is to let the four team members make separate presentations to share in their group. Instead of using PowerPoint presentations in front of the whole class, team members can explain the topic to the group. An example I have is a class working on four well-known authors. Each member of the group gets an author they will study and present to their group. After the agreed time to collect information and material, everyone who has the same author meets across groups to compare what they found and what information they deem essential for this particular author. After this review, everyone goes back to their group and shares. This way, if each group has students who master the subject well, students who struggle with the material will get help.

When the students meet up, they can work on creating a shared presentation. As mentioned, students have a choice between using Office 365, Google Drive, or a OneNote notebook shared in class. That way, absent students have access to the material. And all the presentations will be quality approved. A good option here is to use Movie Maker. The students can easily add audio and music. The presentations can be added to the OneNote Class notebook and, in that way, will be available for all the students, an excellent way to review the material before a test.

Find someone who

This is an exercise in which students interview their peers on a given topic. They can only ask one question per student, and the object is to move around in the classroom until everyone has found the answers or someone gets all the answers first. It is an excellent strategy for the teacher to use when checking for understanding. It can also be an excellent way to get students engaged in what they are about to learn. It can also be used as a way for your students to get to know each other (Figure 5.2).

Example of Find Someone Who

1. _____ Find someone who has a pet.
2. _____ Find someone who has at least one grandparent still alive.
3. _____ Find someone who takes showers instead of baths.
4. _____ Find someone who ate at McDonalds® in the last week.
5. _____ Find someone who drives to school every day.
6. _____ Find someone who owns more than two watches.
7. _____ Find someone who was born south of the equator.
8. _____ Find someone who drank coffee at breakfast today.
9. _____ Find someone who has visited more than five countries.
10. _____ Find someone who speaks more than two languages.
11. _____ Find someone who was born in January.
12. _____ Find someone who has visited Canada.
13. _____ Find someone who is good at math.
14. _____ Find someone who does not like broccoli.
15. _____ Find someone who is an only child.
16. _____ Find someone who likes rice better than potatoes.
17. _____ Find someone who likes pizza.
18. _____ Find someone who likes blue better than red or orange.
19. _____ Find someone who was born in August.
20. _____ Find someone who can swim well.

FIGURE 5.2 An exmaple of "find someone who" for getting to know classmates at the start of the school year.

Send a problem

In send a problem, students work on problem-solving by sharing ideas and input. One way to do this is to have groups of four working on different issues during the same period. Each group receives a problem or a question; the group members then discuss the problems and look for the best possible solutions. In this task, the groups send their suggestions to the other groups for input. To conclude, the groups present a possible solution to the whole class.

Before working on an in-depth individual project, members of the group can write ideas they have and send them to the other members of the group for input. Everyone in the group has to contribute with good ideas on how to solve the task. In the end, each student should have input from three classmates.

Traditionally, this task would be solved by writing on a piece of paper. Today we would typically co-write in a document. Once again, I recommend OneNote, but Google Docs or Office 365 are also good alternatives.

The way of the future

Cooperative learning relies on the principle that we learn better when interacting with others. To achieve this, it is essential for students to learn how to work together. To be able to work well with others is also a required qualification for getting into the job market today. Everyone needs to know how to work in teams and how to collaborate. According to the Organisation for Economic Co-operation and Development (2018), collaboration is a vital skill for students today:

> To prepare for 2030, people should be able to think creatively, develop new products and services, new jobs, new processes and methods, new ways of thinking and living, new enterprises, new sectors, new business models, and new social models. Increasingly, innovation springs not from individuals thinking and working alone, but through cooperation and collaboration with others to draw on existing knowledge to create new knowledge. The constructs that underpin the competency include adaptability, creativity, curiosity, and open-mindedness.

Collaborative learning works best if you spend time establishing well functional groups. Some teachers might think this is too time-consuming, but students learn both faster and better if they thrive in class and feel safe.

Classroom management is essential, and it is a good idea for the teacher to set up the classroom before students enter. In some countries, the teacher has the same classroom every day, but that is not the way in Norway. I usually put the desks together two and two, with plenty of space between the rows. That way, I can easily maneuver around the classroom and talk to all the students. When I want students to work in groups, it is easy for me to form groups of four. Just have the students turn to the pair behind them. Setting up the classroom is especially important in a digital classroom. Sometimes I find desks at the back of the classroom with the chairs close to the wall. It usually means that the students sitting there are not interested in the teacher being able to see what they are doing on their computers. Never let the students decide on the seating arrangement.

References

Bradbury, N. A. (2016). Attention span during lectures: 8 seconds, 10 minutes, or more? *Advances in Physiology Education*, 40(4), 509–513. From the American Physiology Society: https://physiology.org/doi/full/10.1152/advan.00109.2016

Crouch, C. H., Watkins, J., Fagen, A. P., & Mazur, E. (2007). Peer instruction: Engaging students one-on-one, all at once. *Research-Based Reform of University Physics*, 1(1), 1–55.

History of cooperative learning. (n.d.). From K12 Academics: https://www.k12academics.com/education-reform/cooperative-learning/history

Johnson, D. W., & Johnson, R. T. (n.d.). *An overview of cooperative learning.* From What is Cooperative Learning: http://www.co-operation.org/what-is-cooperative-learning

Johnson, D. W., Johnson, R. T., & Stanne, M. (2000). *Cooperative learning methods: A meta-analysis.* Minneapolis: University of Minnesota.

Mueller, P. A., & Oppenheimer, D. M. (2014). The pen is mightier than the keyboard: Advantages of longhand over laptop note taking. *Psychological Science*, 25(6), 1159–1168. From Psychological Science: https://journals.sagepub.com/doi/abs/10.1177/0956797614524581

Organisation for Economic Co-operation and Development. (2018). *The future of education and skills: Education 2030.* Paris: Author.

CHAPTER

6

The flipped classroom

Ann S. Michaelsen

The videos used in a flipped classroom are often made by the teacher, who explains the subject matter and offers examples. The student can watch the videos several times if necessary. In school, time is used to solve problems, often in groups, and everyone has to master the tasks before they can move on. In this chapter we take a closer look at how the teacher can make the videos using the software Explain Everything.

An alternative to making videos is using resources found at the Khan Academy, YouTube, and TED Talks.

Introduction

A traditional way to teach is teachers going through new material with the student at school and then assigning homework. The principle of the flipped classrooms is the opposite: that students get instructions at home in the form of short videos, lasting a maximum of 5 minutes, and work on tasks during school hours. The videos are often made by the teacher, who explains the subject matter and offers examples. The student can watch the video several times if necessary. In school, time is used to solve problems, often in groups, and everyone has to master the tasks before they can move on. You find some examples of the flipped classroom in Chapter 4. This chapter discusses how the use of videos, podcasts, and games all work as well.

The pedagogy behind this

Two teachers from the United States, Aaron Sams and Jonathan Bergmann, were the first to come up with the concept of flipped classrooms. They were both chemistry teachers, and they began collaborating on ways to use technology to improve their face-to-face time with students. They started making videos for the students to watch at home because they wanted the students to have the opportunity to watch instructional videos as many times as they needed to understand the material. Ordinarily, when the teacher explains a topic, many students might not fully understand the content the first time or even the second time, while some get it straight away (Bergmann & Sams, 2012). I first met Johnathan and Aaron at the International Society for Technology in Education conference in Philadelphia, and I asked them over to Norway to speak at our conference in 2012.

A fundamental advantage of the flipped classroom is that the teacher has more time to spend with each student in school. Since students have already seen the instructional video, they can start working with the assignments at school, and the teacher can spend time guiding the students who need help. Flipped classroom works well with cooperative learning, whereby students discuss issues or solve problems after watching the same video at home. In class, the teacher groups students, making sure they all get the help they need.

It is crucial that students only move to the next level when they have understood and mastered the previous one. By using a OneNote notebook, the teacher can see what a student has written and can correct mistakes in the notebook. To help, students can fill out a form explaining the different competency goals and showing the teacher that they master them.

The flipped classroom is best suited for subjects where the teacher needs to explain complex formulas/concepts/rules that students often struggle with and where students' responses are either right or wrong. At our school, we have had great success with the flipped classroom in mathematics and foreign languages (grammar). You can use the principals from the flipped classroom with most curriculum goals that require students to understand complex terminology.

Some teachers are concerned about using this method since they fear that students will not watch the videos at home before they come to school. Students who do not do their homework and come to school unprepared is not a new phenomenon. This method will not miraculously change that, but it will be easier for the teacher to group these students so that they can watch the videos before they start working with tasks in school. The teachers can spend time helping where needed and do not have to spend time going over the material again. The students move on when they are ready.

There are many studies on the effect of the flipped classroom. They show that students are more motivated and engaged when using this method.

In a study "The Flipped Classroom: For Active, Effective and Increased Learning – Especially for Low Achievers," the author found that

> [t]he results revealed that a large majority of the students had a positive attitude towards flipped classroom, the use of video and Moodle, and that a positive attitude towards flipped classroom was strongly correlated to perceptions of increased motivation, engagement, increased learning, and effective learning. Low achievers significantly reported more positively as compared to high achievers with regards to attitudes towards the use of video as a learning tool, perceived increased learning, and perceived more effective learning.
>
> (Nouri, 2016)

In particular, those students who struggle the most with material prefer the flipped classroom.

An essential prerequisite for the success of the flipped classroom is to discuss the material with the class. Discussions in the class, during which students demonstrate mastery and share their solutions with the rest of the class, help increase the learning effect. It is not enough to let students go through video explanations at home and then continue working individually at school. That alone does not give the desired learning effect. Watching the video, taking notes, and then working in groups is what works best.

A study in Norway in 2016 shows that the use of the flipped classroom with cooperative learning can enhance learning:

> We investigated two implementations of the flipped classroom. The first implementation did not actively encourage cooperative learning, with students progressing through the course at their own pace. With this implementation student examination scores did not differ between the lecture classes and the flipped classroom. The second implementation was organised with cooperative learning activities. In a randomised control-group pretest-posttest experiment student scores on a post-test and on the final examination were significantly higher for the flipped classroom group than for the control group receiving traditional lectures. This demonstrates that the classroom flip, if properly implemented with cooperative learning, can lead to increased academic performance.
>
> (Foldnes, 2016)

Classroom application

One thing is to ask students to watch the video at home, but how can you make sure they did? It is a good idea to make a plan with the students when you introduce the flipped classroom. Discuss the advantage of working without social media and other communication channels open. Explain that concentrating on new and difficult concepts requires full attention. It is easy to get distracted. Remind them of the Pomodoro Technique, which is explained in Chapter 8. You should tell the students they can stop the video and rewind if they need to. Students who understand the material typically put the video on a higher speed to browse through it just to make sure they don't miss anything.

Another important point is that students must take notes while watching the videos. They should write down what they understood and any questions they have. It's

---

PRACTICAL EXAMPLES

1. ***Foreign languages*** – Teachers supplement their teaching with videos explaining grammar and conversation starters that students watch before class. Students spend their time at school speaking with other students in the foreign language or, alternatively, use Skype with students in other countries while the teacher walks around and helps. When needed, the teacher asks students to watch some of the videos again.
2. ***Mathematics*** – Instead of the teacher explaining new material on the blackboard/ whiteboard, students are asked to watch a video and take notes at home. The notes will

> indicate if there is a need for clarification. The time at school is used to work on problems and to do assignments in groups with the help of the teacher.
> 3. **English, history, science, religion** – Students see a video in which the teacher presents a particular theme, a problem, a historical event, a religion, or a conflict. Students work on this in groups when they arrive at school and participate in discussions with the rest of the class and the teacher. Before a test, students can revise the material by watching the video again.
> 4. **Physical education** – The teacher provides students with videos to study the rules in sports like soccer, basketball, tennis, dance, and theory and techniques. At school, time is spent applying this knowledge in physical activity.

also a good way for the teacher to see how the video works as a learning tool. Are they all struggling with the illustration. In that case, you know what to change or clarify.

Videos for the flipped classroom

Recording a video is not difficult. And keep in mind that it has to be short – 4 to 5 minutes tops. Teachers who have made videos for their class say that their students prefer to see and hear their teacher explain concepts rather than a "fancy" video with someone they don't know. It doesn't matter if the quality isn't excellent or if you mix up some words now and then. Practice makes perfect. A good idea for getting started is to create a video with a colleague first. Jonathan Bergmann and Aaron Sams, who first came up with this model, made all their videos together. It is easier for the teachers when collaborating and more inspiring for the students. If teachers combine forces, more students will benefit from this. And bear in mind, you do not need anything other than a PC, Mac, or mobile phone.

The content of the videos can be anything from explaining difficult concepts, fact reviews, test reviews, or a "teaser" before a new topic. Another great idea that my colleague at Sandvika High School, Inger-Merethe Nisted, came up with is to post videos with the correct answers immediately after the students take a test. That way, students will get instant feedback. All videos are linked to the curriculum goals and are easily accessible through a YouTube channel. During exams, they can also listen to the videos if they have downloaded them on their computers. At least this is possible in Norway.

When it comes to the actual recording of videos, it is a good idea to make a brief storyboard of the content before starting the recording. There are many ways to capture video for the flipped classroom. Chapter 2 described software that can be used by both students and teachers.

Making videos with Explain Everything

Explain Everything is the fastest-growing interactive whiteboard platform on the market and has been recognized for its excellence in the field by over a dozen organizations (Crunchbase, 2020).

Explain Everything is an application for the IOS iPad, designed to record learning videos. I invited Sigurd A. Michaelsen, a middle school teacher, to write about how he uses this app to create instructional videos in mathematics. The examples he gives can be linked to other subjects as well.

When you start Explain Everything, you'll see a toolbar on the left after opening a new project. Spend some time exploring the tools (Figure 6.1). Here is a brief explanation of the four most important ones:

1. *The pen. The most-used tool in the application. The colors used are black, red, blue, green, and yellow. Together with Apple Pencil on your iPad, this works very well. Remember that you can lean your hand on the tablet while writing.*
2. *Eraser. Use this if you want to remove something without having to undo an entire action. It can be used on both text and images. Zooming in makes it easier.*
3. *Text box. If you need a lot of text, you may want to pull up a keyboard and type it right in.*
4. *Pointer. When recording videos, it is important that students know where to look.*

Explain Everything is also well suited to record entire lessons (Figure 6.2).

Then students can work actively throughout the whole math class as if a private teacher was sitting next to them. Here are some useful points:

1. *Introduce the lesson and topics, and create a clear table of contents so that it is predictable for the students.*
2. *Explain the utensils students need to be active learners. A notebook, pencils, and rulers are some of the tools they need. Explain how they should prepare before the lesson. Write a list of what they need so that they are prepared; otherwise, they will get distracted when they start working.*

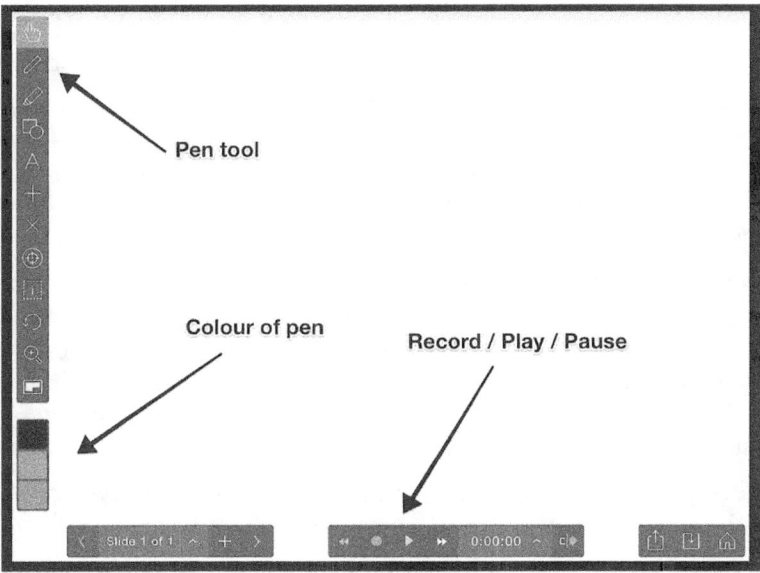

FIGURE 6.1 Explain Everything with a picture of the pen tool, colors, and record, play, and pause.

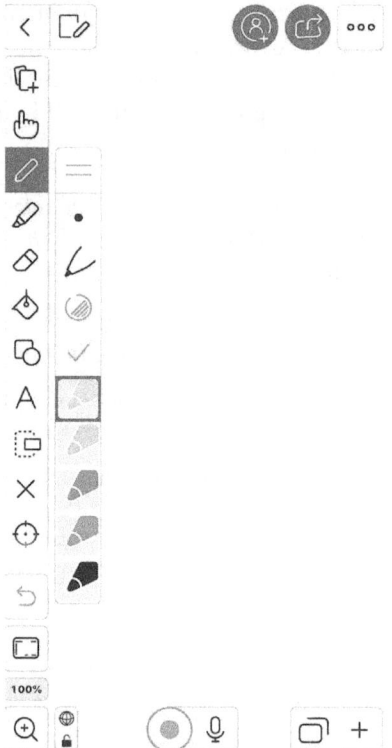

FIGURE 6.2 Explain everything: layout.

3. *List topics to discuss in class after the video. Even if this differs from ordinary whiteboard instruction in front of the whole class, we always have a class review after 20 minutes. Students appreciate this since it is fun to be able to put into words what they have learned immediately after and to check for understanding. Also, it is of great educational value that students can show that they are able to solve math problems and share the solutions with the rest of the class. If students have worked well with the material, they will have the opportunity to solve the problems on the whiteboard. Before I started working like this, only the gifted students were able to do this; now everyone can participate. After I started making videos like this, I have seen a lot more students who want to share what they know in math class.*

4. *Include today's topics and assignments, explanations, and reviews of various tasks with a focus on where to pause. I usually take a screenshot from the textbook so that students see that we are moving forward in the book. The students view the instructions, pause, and do the task. When they are done, they press continue, and then they see how I have solved the task. If they have questions about the tasks, they ask their learning partner. Every student in my math class has a designated learning partner.*

5. *I always post a conclusion part, in which I ask the students to write down any questions they have concerning the video they just watched, what they thought was useful, and*

whether there was something that seemed unclear to them. I have them share this in the same place as where the movie is located. If I see that students have feedback about something that was unclear, I make a video with the explanation. If only one student has questions, I usually get another student to explain. Students who get to help their learning partner always appreciate the opportunity.

> **SOME REMINDERS:**
> - *Speak with confidence and in a clear and distinct voice.*
> - *Only say what is necessary.*
> - *Check and double-check that you have the correct answer. The students take this for granted.*
> - *Do not include anything fancy that might distract the students' attention. Stick to the basics. "Less is more."*

Some teachers need to make a few before they are used to hearing their voice. Don't spend too much time on making your video flawless. Students don't mind if you say a wrong word in the middle of the video as long as you say what was wrong and that you move along quickly.

The Khan Academy

The Khan Academy was founded in 2009 by Sal Khan, who started off in 2006 helping his nephews with math online. The Khan Academy is a nonprofit company, and all Khan Academy courses are free. Students and families just sign up with an email address and password. Many countries have incorporated the material from the Khan Academy, and its lessons are translated into 42 languages.

The Khan Academy offers practice exercises, instructional videos, and a personalized learning dashboard that empower learners to study at their own pace in and outside of the classroom. Khan Academy offers courses in math, science, computing, history, art history, economics, and more (see Figure 6.3). They also offer test preparation content.! See https://www.khanacademy.org/.

YouTube

Many videos found on YouTube can be used in the flipped classroom. Many teachers share their videos with others, and you should consider doing that too. A simple search of "the flipped classroom" gives you a lot of videos to choose from.

It's a good idea to create a YouTube user account and a YouTube channel. Then you'll have all your videos in one place. When you're signed in to your YouTube account, press "+" to add a video to your playlist. YouTube is also a good source of instructional videos for almost every purpose. If you want to find the answer to something, you can search YouTube. Just type in your question.

Math	Math by grade	Science & engineering	Arts & humanities
Early math	Preschool app	Physics	US history
Arithmetic	Kindergarten	AP® Physics 1	AP® US History
Pre-algebra	1st grade	AP® Physics 2	World history
Algebra 1	2nd grade	Cosmology & astronomy	AP® World History
Geometry	3rd grade	Chemistry	US government and civics
Algebra 2	4th grade	AP® Chemistry beta	AP® US Government & Politics
Trigonometry	5th grade	AP® Chemistry	Art history
Precalculus	6th grade	Organic chemistry	AP® Art History
Statistics & probability	7th grade	Biology	Grammar
AP® Calculus AB	8th grade	High school biology	Storytelling
AP® Calculus BC	Illustrative Mathematics	AP® Biology	
AP® Statistics	Eureka Math/EngageNY	Health & medicine	Economics & finance
Multivariable calculus	High school	Electrical engineering	Macroeconomics
Differential equations			AP® Macroeconomics
Linear algebra	Khan Kids app (ages 2-7)	Computing	Microeconomics
	Math, Reading & Social Emotional Learning	Computer programming	AP® Microeconomics
		Computer science	Finance & capital markets
		AP® Computer Science Principles	
		Hour of Code	
		Computer animation	

FIGURE 6.3 A list of what the Khan Academy has to offer.

TED Talks and TED-Ed

TED Talks are influential videos from expert speakers on education, business, science, tech, and so on. Join TED Recommends to get the best ideas, selected just for you. TED is a nonpartisan nonprofit devoted to spreading ideas, usually in the form of short, powerful talks. TED began in 1984 as a conference where Technology, Entertainment, and Design converged, and today covers almost all topics – from science to business to global issues – in more than 110 languages.

(TED, 2020)

The videos are almost always short 18-minute lectures. You will find many lectures here that you can use in your class. I often list videos from TED Talks on my webpage.

TED-Ed is TED's youth and education initiative. TED-Ed's mission is to spark and celebrate the ideas of teachers and students around the world. Everything we do supports learning – from producing a growing library of original animated videos to providing an international platform for teachers to create their own interactive lessons to helping curious students around the globe bring TED to their schools and gain presentation literacy skills, to celebrating innovative leadership within TED-Ed's global network of over 250,000 teachers. TED-Ed has grown from an idea worth spreading into an award-winning education platform that serves millions of teachers and students around the world every week.

(TED-Ed, 2020)

Some points before you start

Whether you choose to create a video, have your students make it, or find a suitable video online, it is important to bear in mind that just watching a video once is not enough. And we all know that students are easily distracted and start using social media, chat with friends, and listen to music. To make this work, certain structures are needed. Spend time talking about study techniques first, and have your students reflect on how they learn best. They need to practice taking relevant notes when watching the videos. It is smart to have them prepare at least one question about what they have learned after the lesson and before they go to class. Questions are good indicators for the teacher regarding whether they have understood the material. You will quickly see if many students are struggling with the same problems.

The truly valuable parts of the flipped classroom are the follow-up questions, problem-solving, and discussions with the students afterward. The big takeaway lies in the teachers spending more time on dialogue with each student and providing the support needed. Some might think this method makes the role of the teachers redundant, but it is actually quite the opposite.

References

Bergmann, J., & Sams, A. (2012). Before you flip, consider this. *Phi Delta Kappan*, 94(6), 25.
Crunchbase. (2020). *Explain everything*. From Crunchbase: https://www.crunchbase.com/organization/explain-everything
Foldnes, N. (2016, March 17). The flipped classroom and cooperative learning: Evidence from a randomised experiment. *Active Learning in Higher Education*, 17(1), 39–49.
Nouri, J. (2016, August 24). The flipped classroom: For active, effective and increased learning – especially for low achievers. *International Journal of Education Technology in Higher Education*, 13, Article 33.
TED. (2020). *TED ideas worth spreading*. From TED: https://www.ted.com/
TED-Ed. (2020). *About TED-Ed*. From TED-Ed: https://ed.ted.com/about

CHAPTER 7

Teaching with video games

Aleksander Husøy and Tobias Staaby

Introduction

As teachers and specialists in game pedagogy at Nordahl Grieg Upper Secondary School, we have spent the last 10 years exploring the relatively uncharted waters that are games and learning. Our yearning for discovery has been a personal one. Video games have been a part of our lives since childhood, and bringing this medium into the classroom was as obvious a choice as textbooks, film, or literature.

In this chapter, we want to share some of the discoveries in the pedagogical use of video games that we have made so far. Before we move on, we should clarify that teaching with games is not a single method. Games can be approached in the classroom in a multitude of ways. In this chapter, we cover three of these perspectives: (1) learning with games – building awareness of what roles video games can have as tools for teaching and learning, (2) learning about games – video games are cultural artifacts worthy of study and can be analyzed and compared with other forms of expression, and (3) games as vicarious, firsthand experiences – using games as digital field trips or role-play to experience situations otherwise inaccessible within the classroom. There is some overlap between these perspectives, and learning units that incorporate games might contain elements of all three perspectives.

The educational affordances of video games

In this chapter, we argue that games should not be regarded as educational artifacts in and of themselves but, rather, as tools for teaching and learning. In other words, games are only as useful to us, and our students, as the opportunities for meaning, action, and learning they afford us. Games are potentially valuable for educational contexts not for what they are but for what affordances they bring to the table.

The term *affordance* is a somewhat ambiguous term (Harwood & Hafezieh, 2017). In this chapter, we define *affordance* as the relationship between the properties of the object and the abilities and knowledge of the subject (Norman, 2013, p. 11). This means that a given object presents different affordances to different individuals. A cardboard box offers you a place to store your things while offering your cat a place to have a nap. A skilled mountain climber will probably find different affordances in a rock wall than someone who gets out of breath after a few flights of stairs. Some affordances are also more useful or relevant, depending on the context. A ladder affords climbing but is only useful to us if we, for instance, are painting the outside walls of our house or are struggling to reach a particularly high place. Sunscreen affords protection from getting sunburned but is of is of little use in a snowstorm in the middle of December.

This means that the educational affordances of video games are sensitive both to the actors in the classroom – the teacher and the students – and to the particular classroom context. What subject are we teaching? What are the learning goals? How familiar are we and our students with the game? What skills, knowledge, and hardware do we need to play it? What can the player learn from playing the game, and how can we make this curricular relevant? How can we use elements of video games to facilitate different learning activities?

The educational affordances of a video game present themselves on two different levels. The first level – what we would call the "classroom level" – concerns how the game as a whole serves as a mediating artifact in social and educational activities in the classroom in the same way one would use other artifacts, such as calculators, textbooks, documentaries, laptops, tablets, presentational tools, and so on. The classroom level concerns what assignments, questions, discussions, and other learning activities the game affords our students and us. We can analyze and discuss the accuracy of a game's portrayal of a historical event, use dilemmas from a game as a basis for a classroom discussion, ask students to compare a game's presentation of a phenomenon to how the phenomenon appears in real life, use the game as inspiration for creative writing, use a game as a catalyst for other oral or written assignments and activities, and so on. Games can afford a multitude of different classroom activities, but these affordances are dependent on the teacher's and the students' knowledge and abilities, the classroom context, and the subject matter at hand.

The other level on which the game presents affordances – what we call the "gameplay level" – regards the game as its own environment, where the player controls a virtual body (often referred to as an "avatar"), meets virtual characters, uses virtual tools in virtual environments, and experiences virtual events. In other words, the game is no longer viewed as a whole but as a conglomerate of virtual objects and entities. Affordances at the game level depend on not only the skills and abilities of the player but also on the qualities of the avatar the player is controlling, as well as whatever virtual environment they find themselves in and what virtual tools they have access to. Super Mario's ability to make a jump or defeat an enemy depends both on the player and Mario himself. If Mario collects a power-up, like a Fire Flower, both Mario's and the player's abilities will change. This also means that whatever skills and knowledge the player gains from the gameplay is primarily useful in a gameplay context. While it is true that games are excellent at presenting the player with the right knowledge at the right time, this is almost always directed at reaching in-game goals. Learning to defeat an enemy, traverse an obstacle, or achieve an objective are the first and foremost gameplay activities and do not automatically translate into knowledge about the world outside the game.

It is essential that we are mindful of this relationship between the virtual and the real, between the classroom level and the gameplay level. One way to think about this is that games at a classroom level concern learning with games, while the gameplay level is about learning in games. This means that the learning taking place in a game is not necessarily transferable to real-life situations. For instance, a player might encounter a low wall in a game that looks perfectly climbable and make the perfectly reasonable assumption that this wall offers climbing only to find out that it does not. The affordance that then appears is not one of traversal but one of hindrance. As the perceived affordance of the wall turns out to be false, the meaning the player sees in the wall also changes. The virtual wall does not have the properties a similar, real-life wall would have. If this can be said of simple objects like a wall, it is even more of an issue with more complex objects and phenomena like chemical processes, historical periods, or societal institutions.

That is not to say that learning does not happen during gameplay, or that transfer of knowledge from gameplay to other contexts is impossible. After all, a game designer can create as realistic virtual representations of real-world objects and phenomena as possible, and in those instances, the problem of transfer might be less of an issue. Our point is that we can't automatically assume that this transfer happens or that nothing is lost in translation. This also means that we should never assume learning goals are achieved through gameplay alone – this goes for both educational and commercial video games. It is important to bookend a gameplay session with pre- and post-activities, such as discussion, written assignments, and the like. The intent is to position gameplay within a curricular perspective, as well as help students use their gameplay experiences as a resource for thinking, talking, writing, and, most important, learning. As a result of this, we argue that the use of video games for teaching and learning should be done with considerations of how educational affordances at a gameplay level and a classroom level are and can be connected. Gameplay experiences and learning at the game level are, of course, also necessary – after all, what good is a game if we don't play it? But for gameplay experiences to become resources for learning, they have to be framed by pre- and post-gameplay learning activities at a classroom level.

Games as cultural artifacts

At this point in history, it ought not be controversial to state that games, like film and literature, are significant cultural artifacts. Like other forms of cultural expression, games can tell stories, evoke emotional reactions, and convey values or ideas. This should not be understood to mean that all games have equal value. Games are as different in content and complexity as *The Great Gatsby* is different from The Baby-Sitters Club book series. Schools serve an important function in exposing students to a variety of cultural expressions. This includes assisting students in building the competence to appreciate more complex cultural expressions. Although students may read novels at home, we study novels in schools to expand our students' horizons from simple entertainment to great works of literature.

Many students spend a significant amount of time playing video games outside of school, but for many of these students, their game diet consists primarily of easily accessible entertainment. We believe that schools should be an arena where the depth and breadth of the game medium should be explored, much in the way we explore novels.

As public institutions, schools are in a unique position to provide insight into the variety of cultural expressions that can be found within the game genre. Games are, after all, much more than button mashing and high scores. They are cultural expressions that contain many of the features of traditional media with some additional traits that are specific to video games.

Literature allows us to walk a mile in another person's shoes and to see the world through their eyes. Video games also give us these affordances, but in addition to that, they also allow for the agency to make decisions in their world. In games, we can experience the life of a civilian in a war-torn city; we can feel the suffering of parenting a child dying from cancer and a whole range of other situations that may be far distant from the player's day-to-day life. While novels and films may show us these stories, games make the player an active decision-maker and participant. This agency creates an even stronger bond between player and game than between reader and novel.

Video gaming is a pastime more popular among youth than the general population. Nonplaying teachers might be dazzled by the game competence demonstrated by the young and thereby believe they have little to contribute if games were brought into the classroom. It is, however, important to be aware that there is a distinction between being operationally competent and game literacy. It will seldom be useful for novice-gaming teachers to strive to become more operationally competent than their students. The role of teachers is to convey game literacy – understanding games as socially constructed cultural artifacts with implicit and explicit values. Thankfully, this does not require the teacher to be an expert button-masher.

Games as role-play and digital field trips

The last perspective we would like to introduce is to regard games as a source of meaningful firsthand experiences. It involves using games with the intent of affording students with vicarious (albeit simulated, fictional, and virtual) experiences with events, concepts, and phenomena that would otherwise remain abstract and impalpable. Games can help reify curricular content in a way that, when used in parallel with instruction, discussion, and other activities, can provide different modalities and serve as a mediational tool for learning about a phenomenon, concept, or subject. There's also evidence to suggest that video game experiences can aid student retention (Nishikawa & Jaeger, 2011).

Whether games are used as role-playing exercises or as digital field trips, the gameplay experience is the central part of the educational design. Here, both teaching and learning are oriented toward the actions the player, or players, take in the game, why and how they do these actions, and the experiences that arise from these actions. In general terms, we can think of field trips as bringing the class out into the world and role-play as bringing the world into the classroom. They are by no means mutually exclusive – a role-playing exercise can be part of a field trip and vice versa. Indeed, in games, these often go hand in hand: By stepping into the role of the main character, the player is also stepping into another world.

A key difference between games as role-play and games as digital field trips is that role-play is more concerned with the characters we inhabit and the actions we take, whereas field trips are more about the places, environments, and settings we visit. Again, these often go hand in hand in video games. Therefore, the perspective we wish to emphasize has more to do with the subject matter and learning goals than with the video game itself. Do you want the students to learn and talk about how it might have been to live at a particular time in history or how to make ethical judgments from another person's point of view? Take a role-playing perspective. Are the learning goals more about understanding a period in time, a physical or chemical process, or about other events or processes? If so, a digital field trip is probably a better approach.

As noted earlier in this chapter, the degree to which video games simulate and represent reality faithfully can vary greatly. Whether this is an issue for using games as teaching tools depends on what we wish to teach and how we want to use games when doing so. In a subject like chemistry or physics, the game should have a somewhat accurate representation of the relevant processes (although if this is not the case, we can always task our students with accounting for any discrepancies in the game's representation of reality). If we are teaching a subject like ethics, the most important factor is that the characters in the game are relatable and possible to empathize with and that the game affords well-designed dilemmas with no simple or obvious solutions. In a subject such as history, the game needs to contain sufficient relevant historical information – if the game presents a counterfactual history, it needs to overlap with the actual history so that it is possible to place it in a given period and so on. In short, the game does not need to contain a completely faithful representation of reality, but the relevant parts need to be recognizable enough that teachers and students are able to make connections between the game and the subject matter.

No matter the perspective, much of the potential for using games in this way lies in drawing parallels from the students' gameplay experiences to real-world contexts and situations. We argue that this is not so much a process of transfer, as we've already argued against, as it is a process of translation. Games might be similar to reality, but they are not the same as reality; they are merely representations of reality created by other people. Nevertheless, they afford students with simplified versions of reality that can highlight the most relevant elements of the subject matter while toning down factors that are of less importance, thus making learning goals easier to achieve.

However, how the teacher frames the gameplay experience in a curricular context is crucial, and the teacher should encourage the students to question the games' portrayal of reality and be mindful of both similarities and differences. Crossing this "reality gap" from game to reality can be a valuable learning experience for the students, as long as the teacher is there to aid them. This translation process can be done through classroom discussions, written assignments, and other learning activities. Students can focus on the actions they do in-game, the game's narrative and events, its different themes or other elements, or a combination of these. The most important factor is that students are focused on the curriculum-relevant game elements and that they make the necessary connections between gameplay experience and subject matter.

As noted earlier, the relevant elements of the game depend on the subject matter and learning goals at hand. In physics and other scientific subjects, learning goals can be oriented toward the players' actions in games containing simulations of the laws of physics or other deterministic processes. In language teaching or in social science, it would make more sense to direct students' attention toward how the game represents a certain phenomenon, concept, or term on a more literary, aesthetic, or semantic level. Games that contain ethical and emotional dilemmas are better suited to social science or moral philosophy, but if these games also contain a narrative element, they might be suited to subjects in which students express their interpretations of the narrative events, fictional characters, and the basis for their own actions.

Games in the classroom

In this section, we present some concrete ideas for how games can be implemented in the classroom. These examples are based on lesson units that we have used with our students during the last few years. All the games mentioned in this section are commercial, "off-the-shelf" games that were not designed to be used in the classroom. View these examples as models of how these games might be used. Each teacher will need to make adaptations to make the lessons suitable for their specific classroom.

PEGI ratings: The games in this section have the following PEGI ratings:

Democracy 3	−3
Gone Home	−15
My Child: Lebensborn	−12
Plague Inc.	−7

PEGI is the video game rating system used in most European countries. The ratings indicate age suitability, not the level of difficulty. Teachers who want to make use of a game with a higher PEGI rating than the age of their students should consult parents and school administrators before making use of the game.

Access to technology varies greatly from one school to the next. Teachers need to consider possible technological barriers to making use of these or other video games. For the games mentioned in this section, to have just a single copy of the game is sufficient for Democracy 3 and Plague Inc. The class can make decisions collectively with the gameplay projected for the entire classroom. For Gone Home and My Child: Lebensborn, you will need one device with the game installed per two students.

Role-play and simulation – Democracy 3

Democracy 3 is a simulation of political decision-making in which the player is tasked with changing or implementing new laws. Every decision has a range of consequences for various groups in society. To succeed in the game, the interests of individuals, groups, and the state as a whole need to be weighed against each other before decisions are made. For instance, a player might choose to increase alcohol taxes. This will lead to an increase in state revenue, support from religious voters, and a decrease in the consumption of alcohol. On the other hand, it also creates displeasure in other voting groups and may cause an outcry from corporate interests.

The game can be used in social studies as a tool to study the process of political decision making and how these are shaped by the culture and values of different countries. Democracy 3 can also be used as a framework for model parliamentary role-play. When using a single copy of the game projected on the board, students can be divided into groups to discuss and vote on policy decisions.

Democracy 3 is a complex game with an interface that is not always intuitive to the novice player. This can be an obstacle if students were to play the game individually. However, when the game is used in whole-class play, students do not need to be experts on the game mechanics. The students can focus on learning the policy interests of their party and creating strategies to negotiate these interests. The teacher (or a game-literate student) can input the class's decisions into the game.

Games as narratives – Gone Home

Gone Home takes fewer than 4 hours to play and is easy to use even for teachers and students with limited gaming experience. The player takes on the role of a young woman who, after a year abroad, returns to her family home. The house is abandoned, and through exploring the house and artifacts found within, the story of what has happened to her family can be revealed. The player is free to navigate the house at her own pace. Although parts of the story are revealed in a different order in separate playthroughs, the components of the story remain the same regardless of player choice.

With the important exception of player choice, the game has a structure similar to short stories, which makes planning learning activities similar to those one would plan for work with other literature. Gone Home can be analyzed for its narrative techniques, plot, and character development or be compared and contrasted with narratives in more familiar genres. The game is rich in references and imagery of the American West Coast in the 1990s and deals with themes like coming of age, sexual identity, and otherness.

Games as digital field trips – My Child: Lebensborn

In the British Academy of Film and Television Arts–award-winning My Child: Lebensborn, the player takes on the role of a foster parent for a 7-year-old child in postwar Norway. The child was fathered by a German soldier and has been abandoned by its biological mother. In a society where the scars from World War II are still far from healed, you are tasked with giving this child a safe upbringing.

Although game mechanics of My Child: Lebensborn are simple, the game tells a compelling story about growing up in a society that does not accept you as well as of a parent's grief of not being able to shield its child from the disdain of society. Through uncomplicated actions like playing, feeding, and talking to the child, a relationship is built not only between the characters within the game but also between the characters and the player interacting with them. This emotional connection can be used as a starting point to discuss the plight of children of war. It can also be used to explore a range of other issues such as bullying, childhood poverty, discrimination, and racism.

My Child: Lebensborn can be played on mobiles or tablets, which in many cases will make this game more accessible to the classroom than other games acknowledged in this chapter. The game raises an often overlooked part of Norwegian history, but the themes it raises are applicable to the marginalization of other groups either in the past or the present. The game takes approximately 5 hours to complete, but depending on the lesson unit, it will often be sufficient with 1 to 2 hours of game time. My Child: Lebensborn can be a useful game to supplement other resources in subjects such as social science and history. It can also be valuable in vocational training courses in the fields of youth work and child care.

Games as simulations – Plague Inc.

In Plague Inc., you control a pathogen – a virus, a bacterium, or other nasty things – whose sole purpose is to wipe out the world's population. While the player has little or no control over where the disease will spread, they have great control over the disease's symptoms and how it infects its victims. The player can also choose the country in which the disease first starts infecting humans. If you want a challenge, choose a well-developed country with solid health services and good infrastructure; for a significantly easier start, you should choose a poor, highly populated developing country. The game is available for both mobile, PC, and tablets.

While the game might seem a bit macabre to some, the game can be a great utility for talking, teaching, and learning about how diseases spread. The game is best suited for science subjects concerning pathology and evolution, but one can also use the game in mathematics, for example, by making models or other representations of how quickly the disease spreads. Furthermore, the game contains design elements and choices, which could also make for excellent discussion topics regarding how the game represents the world and the degree to which this is an accurate representation. The elements are, for instance, how the game presents some countries as more resistant to infection and the fact that a recent update introduced anti-vaxxers as a game element. Future versions of the game will include a game mode where the player actively fights against the spread of the disease rather than controlling it.

Important considerations

Access to devices varies greatly between schools and school systems, but even in schools with 1:1 access to devices, we generally recommend using games in the classroom as a shared experience, either in pairs or in whole-class play. A significant benefit of using games in class is the discussions that can be had while experiencing a game. If students are playing by themselves, many will rush through games to reach the win-state as quickly as possible. This is not conducive to students reflecting on how the game relates to the learning objectives for the lesson.

When students play in pairs, game progression is slower, which creates space to consider their choices in the game and how these relate to the concepts they are working on in class. Teachers should not only ensure students are able to explore the game at their own pace but also provide tasks or discussion prompts to help students bridge what is happening in the game with the learning content of that lesson.

Depending on what choices students make in the game, it can be much more difficult for teachers to be aware of how students are progressing. This is a significant difference between games and traditional "non-interactive" media. If students are assigned to read a novel up until a certain point, the teacher can be reasonably certain that the entire class is on the same page. Different players may have made very different choices and thereby have very different experiences than one had anticipated. For this reason, teachers who use games in their classes need to be extraordinarily flexible to adapt accordingly during the lesson.

This does not mean that students should be absolutely free to use the game any way they want. Before running a game unit, one needs to have a clear plan for progression and to have considered to what extent students should be guided in their decision-making. Independent play will give students a more authentic game experience, but some guidelines are essential to keep them focused on the lesson objectives. Finding the right balance is one of the more challenging aspects of teaching with games. There is no single correct approach that will be ideal in all contexts, but we strongly encourage teachers to make use of the same games in different groups and adapt based on their experiences.

We hope this chapter has given you some new insights into what learning with games is and can be. We encourage all teachers to explore both these and other games and consider what benefits they might bring to your classroom, especially those teachers who do not consider themselves as gamers. Computer games can be a lot more useful and a loss let complicated than many teachers might think.

Final words of advice

- Before you bring a game into the classroom – play it yourself. Ensure that you have the necessary technology and equipment available.
- Remember that games are active media (unlike books or film) in which students take part in controlling the action. Make full use of these interactive possibilities.
- You set the goals for the unit. Help your students stay focused on your goals rather than the goals set by the game.
- Do not fear failure! Students may be more competent in game mechanics than you are – make use of this. Your role is to assist students in understanding the game in relation to your subject, let students take charge of tech support.

References

Harwood, S. A., & Hafezieh, N. (2017). *'Affordance' – What does this mean? Presentation at the Proceedings of 22nd UKAIS, Annual Conference,* April 3–5, 2015, St Catherine's College, Oxford, England.

Nishikawa, K. A., & Jaeger, J. (2011). A computer simulation comparing the incentive structures of dictatorships and democracies. *Journal of Political Science Education,* 7(2), 135–142.

Norman, D. (2013). *The design of everyday things: Revised and expanded edition.* New York, NY: Basic Books.

CHAPTER

8

Digital citizenship

Ann S. Michaelsen

Introduction

According to the Organisation for Economic Co-operation and Development (OECD, 2018),

> [e]mpowering an active and ethical digital generation means equipping children to actively, positively, and responsibly engage in society, whether this takes place on or offline. Digital citizenship can be understood as norms of behavior regarding the use of digital technologies. Digital citizenship involves:
>
> - competent and positive engagement with digital technology (access and skills)
> - active and responsible participation (empowerment and etiquette)
> - lifelong learning in formal, non-formal, and informal contexts (including risk management and resilience).

Countries have taken different approaches to foster the development of digital citizenship in their students. As engaging with digital technologies comes with risks, children must be empowered with the tools and information needed to navigate digital environments in an ethical and responsible way. This includes knowing how to identify, anticipate, and react effectively to risks, for example, cyberbullying and threats to security and privacy.

With our extensive use of technology comes the need for new ways of thinking, new knowledge, and new challenges. I think we can all agree that we need young people who are critical, explorative, and creative. Critical thinking and being able to find reliable sources are both vital components of digital citizenship and are particularly important in our culture of Facebook shares and likes. The internet is a global arena where everyone can participate in exchanging opinions and ideas. It is, therefore, essential that students can question the information they find online. In other words, we need informed citizens who know what to share and what to ignore. If not, our democracy will suffer and be undermined. We have seen many examples of this in elections. Google "interfering in elections," and you will see. School plays an important role here. Young people need to learn how to behave online and be aware of the dangers they may encounter. Only then can they become competent digital citizens and by that use the web to strengthen democracy instead of destroying it. It is the teacher's job to discuss this with their students. There are many ways to ensure that the information you find online is accurate and realiable. In Figures 8.1 and 8.2, you will see that the first results in the search have a checkbox next to them. I have used a service called Newsguard, which is explained later in this chapter.

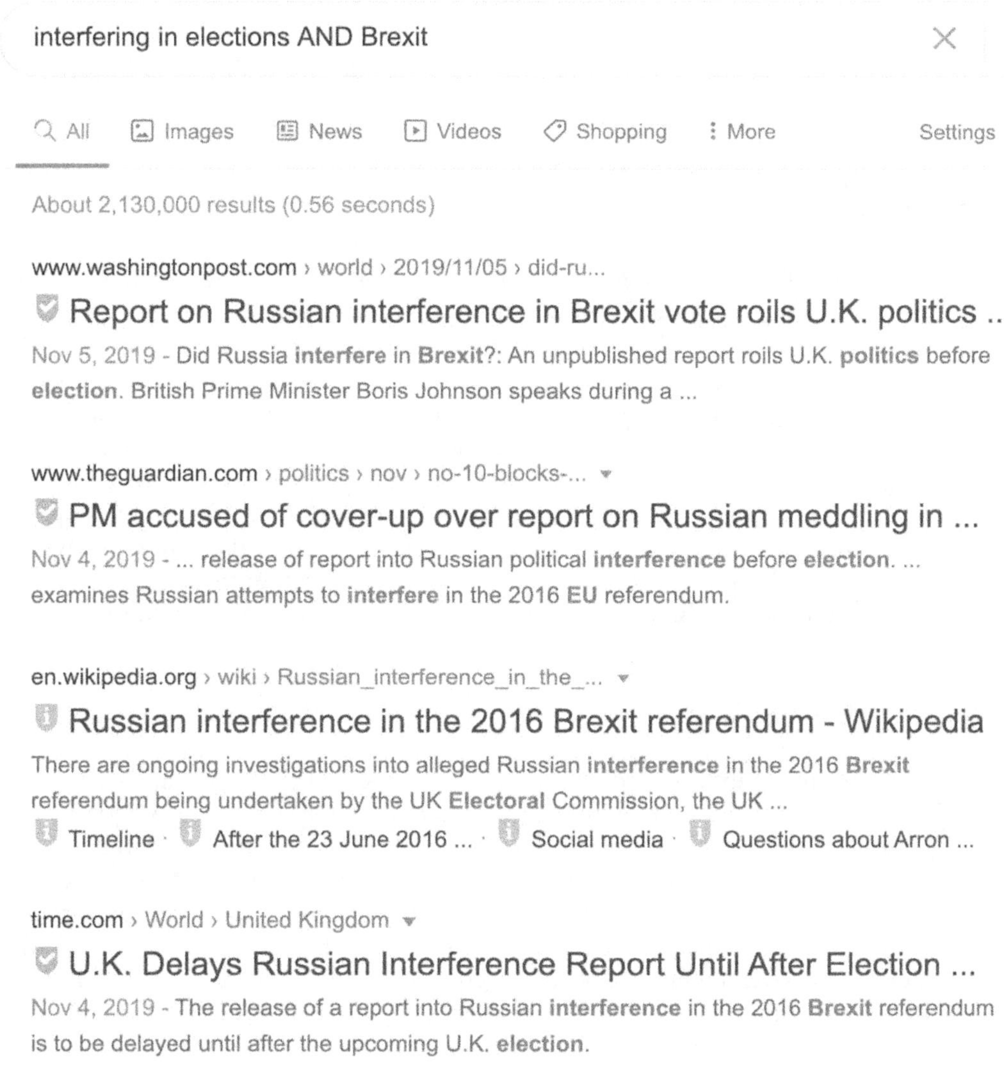

interfering in elections AND Brexit

All   Images   News   Videos   Shopping   More   Settings

About 2,130,000 results (0.56 seconds)

www.washingtonpost.com › world › 2019/11/05 › did-ru...
Report on Russian interference in Brexit vote roils U.K. politics ..
Nov 5, 2019 - Did Russia **interfere** in **Brexit**?: An unpublished report roils U.K. **politics** before **election**. British Prime Minister Boris Johnson speaks during a ...

www.theguardian.com › politics › nov › no-10-blocks-... ▼
PM accused of cover-up over report on Russian meddling in ...
Nov 4, 2019 - ... release of report into Russian political **interference** before **election**. ... examines Russian attempts to **interfere** in the 2016 **EU** referendum.

en.wikipedia.org › wiki › Russian_interference_in_the_... ▼
Russian interference in the 2016 Brexit referendum - Wikipedia
There are ongoing investigations into alleged Russian **interference** in the 2016 **Brexit** referendum being undertaken by the UK **Electoral** Commission, the UK ...
Timeline · After the 23 June 2016 ... · Social media · Questions about Arron ...

time.com › World › United Kingdom ▼
U.K. Delays Russian Interference Report Until After Election ...
Nov 4, 2019 - The release of a report into Russian **interference** in the 2016 **Brexit** referendum is to be delayed until after the upcoming U.K. **election**.

FIGURE 8.1 Searching for "interference in elections AND Brexit".

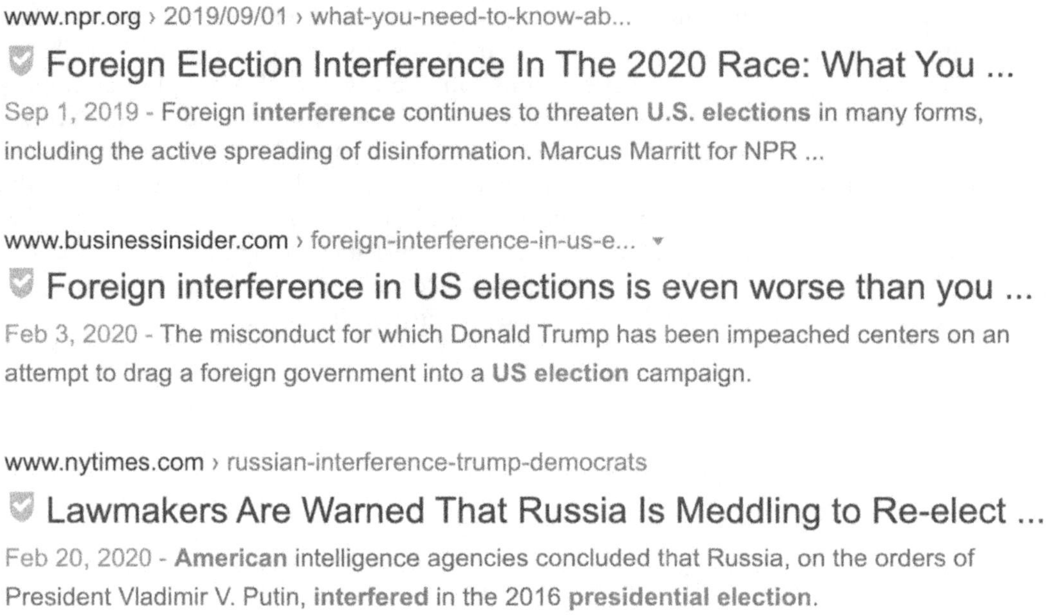

www.npr.org › 2019/09/01 › what-you-need-to-know-ab...
Foreign Election Interference In The 2020 Race: What You ...
Sep 1, 2019 - Foreign **interference** continues to threaten **U.S. elections** in many forms, including the active spreading of disinformation. Marcus Marritt for NPR ...

www.businessinsider.com › foreign-interference-in-us-e... ▼
Foreign interference in US elections is even worse than you ...
Feb 3, 2020 - The misconduct for which Donald Trump has been impeached centers on an attempt to drag a foreign government into a **US election** campaign.

www.nytimes.com › russian-interference-trump-democrats
Lawmakers Are Warned That Russia Is Meddling to Re-elect ...
Feb 20, 2020 - **American** intelligence agencies concluded that Russia, on the orders of President Vladimir V. Putin, **interfered** in the 2016 **presidential election**.

FIGURE 8.2 Searching for "interference in US elections".

We can call what is required "digital discernment." Digital discernment is learning critical thinking to thwart disinformation. Essential components are copyright rules and what you can publish about others without asking for permission. This is also what we could call "information competence," the ability to find and assess relevant information. The goal of becoming information competent is to empower decision-making in the course of problem-solving by uncovering meaning. It is equally imperative that students can evaluate their use of digital tools, and by that, I mean how to know what to use and when to use it. Students are often better than teachers when it comes to playing online games or using social media, but they aren't always able to choose the right tools to learn. In this chapter, I try to address some of the challenges on how to behave online and how to avoid distractions when learning online.

How to behave online?

There are many examples of bullying online, and mistakes happen. Even when we know that what we post online most certainly will stay online, sometimes forever. Regardless of how common it is to use social media, we have to remember that a "like" or a "share" of a rude remark online can have devastating consequences. There are, unfortunately, many examples of bad judgment online that have had catastrophic results for those involved. Digital judgment is taught by providing students with confidence and competence to become responsible and reflected citizens. It is about establishing ethical awareness, as well as actual skills that enable learners to safeguard their privacy and that of others.

"Digital footprint" is a metaphor most students can relate to. A digital footprint is a trail of data you create while using the internet. It includes the websites you visit, emails you send, and the information you submit to online services. A "passive digital footprint" is data you leave behind, most times unintentionally. Many forget that being online means sharing in a public space, and they do not know how quickly images and comments can go viral. The prospect of retracting such information is almost nonexistent. We can also see examples of adults posting comments they later regret; even politicians have made fatal remarks on Facebook. Students may find that a "friend" takes a screenshot of an image they posted on Snapchat. Not everyone is aware of the impact a post like that can have, not only for the intended victim but also for the one who shared it.

In other words, students must learn to think more than twice before they publish. A golden rule is that if you are uncertain about who should see your post, don't publish. And that goes for Snapchat and Instagram too. You never know what can happen to it later. This is simply about protocol, manners, and treating people with respect. We all have responsibilities here, but schools have an even greater responsibility, in my opinion. In other words, teachers should be cautious about comments they post and remember to set an example of how to behave online.

Teachers need to discuss this with their students. With 24/7 access to mobile phones, tablets, and PCs, it's tempting to be online all the time. Remember to be careful with what you share. Maybe you will regret it later? What if it is shared online by someone you do not know? I guess we all have read horror stories about how an innocent comment can ruin young people's lives. And that does not only include comments but also pictures and hateful statements. As a teacher, there are many pitfalls, even an innocent nickname when playing Kahoot in class can be hurtful. Seemingly harmless comments on a Padlet could also have devastating effects. The problem with violating other people online is that the comments are visible, accessible, and shareable. A seemingly innocent comment can have consequences. It is a good idea to think carefully before writing anything online. A good recommendation for students might be to answer the questions, Is it okay that everyone I know reads this? Would I show this to my parents? and will I be okay if someone reads this, years from now?

Classroom application

Questions about how to behave online are linked to how students are perceived online. What will a future employer find if he or she Googles you? Is it necessarily a good thing if Google turns nothing up? Today, your online activity can be viewed as a curriculum vitae for future jobs. If you are active in politics or humanitarian work or are a volunteer at school, that might be a good thing to share. Be a positive, responsible digital citizen online. Try to Google your name now and then. Teachers should as well. It is smart.

Consequences of sharing pictures online

How many of you have shared a photo on social media without asking permission? When posting a picture of family or friends, you should always ask first. My experience is that more and more parents are careful about posting pictures of their children, even if it is just an innocent picture of children playing. Much more dangerous are all the images that were taken in a moment of regret and were easily shared and spread online. I'm talking about nude pictures or pictures of friends who have had too much to drink. Very many, if not all, regret having taken them and have a hard time when the photos are shared online. The consequences of sharing can also become extremely uncomfortable for those involved. It is important to inform young people that saving and sharing nude photos of others without consent is punishable by law and that the penalty level for this is high – at least it is in Norway. In some instances, you may be punished at a later date if you share images even if you have been given consent from the people in the picture at the time taken. At a later date, it could turn out to be almost impossible to prove that you have consent, and it might be useful to know that you are the one who has to prove it. The most straightforward advice is, therefore, don't share nude photos of other people – and if someone shares with you, delete them.

I know many parents are afraid of their kids meeting strangers online, but many of the stories we hear about are about young people who already know each other. It is essential to be able to talk about this, and if young people think they have done something stupid, they need an adult they trust.

Class discussions

There are many examples of online bullying. It might have started with an innocent comment. My advice to teachers is to spend some time talking with students about this. I have listed some ways you can address this in your class. I recommend using cooperative learning structures (see Chapter 5). Group your students in fours and let them discuss the different topics that follow. Many online places offer advice. Google has a website called Be Internet Awesome. And it offers Digital Safety Resources to share in class (Google, 2020).

> **For primary school teachers**, it's a good idea to talk about what kids are doing online. In 2016, Facebook, Snapchat, Instagram, and Kik were the most used social media among Norwegian 9- to 16-year-olds. Some of these sites require usernames and passwords, and there are also sites with age restrictions. That could be a problem since many children share usernames and passwords with their friends. Few are aware of the consequences if children log on to a friend's account and pretend to be someone else. It is also smart to remind students, even the young ones, that if they have a photo of a friend, they need to ask first if it is okay to share it. If there is a picture of a person under the age of 15, they have to ask the parents first. At least in Norway, they do. An exception is pictures of activities where the activity is an important part, and there are many people in the picture. An example could be a soccer game.
>
> There are websites like goSupermodel, primarily aimed at young girls. How many in the class use sites like that? Another topic to discuss is if the students have rules for using the internet at home and school. How much use is okay?
>
> **Use of online nicknames.** Does anyone in the class use a secret nickname? If so, why? Do students log on to sites with an age limit? Has anyone ever regretted something they have done online? If so, what did they do then? Ask the students if they can talk to their parents if they experience something online that they know or think is wrong? What is proper online etiquette, and what are suitable passwords?

For high school teachers, work with case studies in your class. The following are some examples of case studies.

Students sit in groups of four and discuss the six following allegations. Based on the discussions, each group creates a poster with rules for internet use.
1   You get a photo, and you know that the person in the picture doesn't want anyone to see it. What do you do?
2   What can the penalty be if you pass it on to someone else?
3   Do you share pictures of yourself that you do not want everyone to see?
4   Have you considered that someone you trust today might be mad at you for some reason and pass on private pictures?
5   How do you react if someone you know is sharing pictures that are not meant to be shared?

How to search online

An essential part of digital discernment is knowing where to find information and knowing which sources you can trust.

Many teachers are surprised that students do not know how to search for information. They do not have the necessary skills. They can easily find information about movies and music online, and they are indeed very good at shopping and finding great deals. Then why is it that even if students know that they should get information from separate sources, they usually settle with the top one or two results they get in a search?

This is where the teacher needs to be a role model. It is time to reflect on how you search for information. Most people settle for the first three results and do not narrow down their search words. Does that apply to you? No point in complaining about students' ability to search online if teachers do not know how to search in a smart way. I suggest teachers take time to show students how to perform a smart search. How to use multiple search engines, broaden their search, and conduct advanced searches by adding filters. Specific guidance and instructions on how to do this are found in Chapter 2.

Explain how and why Google finds results. Search engines like Google, Bing, and Yahoo are free of charge because our searches give them information about what interests us. Many of the search engines also collaborate with Facebook and Instagram, so everything you do online leaves traces between applications. Our searches are not a private matter. Google does not sell your personal information to anyone. It uses the data to serve you relevant ads in Google products, on partner websites, and in mobile apps. These ads help fund the services and make them free for everyone.

Google advertising, or pay-per-click advertising, is a marketing technique that puts online ads in search engine results. Businesses that place these advertisements in the search results pay a small amount of money every time a user clicks on one of their ads. This form of advertising has proved to be a lot more powerful because people who use search engines to buy stuff reveal a lot about their intention – what they want to buy or when they are ready to buy.

Author and teacher Howard Rheingold has an excellent example of this in his book. (Rheingold, 2012) When British Petroleum (BP) had its big oil spill in the Gulf of Mexico in 2010, it bought sponsored links with all major search engines. When searching for "oil spill," "BP's oil spill," or "Deepwater Horizon," its links came up at the top. In that way, BP tried to control the information flow concerning the accident.

Google's business model also influences information searches when we are looking for information to use at school. Google gives you the information they think you want, not necessarily the information that you need. Google wants us to get information tailored to our taste and shopping habits. That way, it ensures that its customers continue to use its services (and so it will keep making money). If you search for news about Egypt and have just searched for a holiday, you might get holiday destinations in Egypt if you forget to add a specific search word. This personalized tailoring might be a good thing when searching for merchandise to buy but will give you little if you are looking to learn about complicated issues from different viewpoints. Learning is, by definition, a meeting with something you did not know, had not thought about, or could not imagine was possible. In other words, a Google search will not move you beyond your familiar comfort zone. This is what Eli Pariser (2011) calls the "filter bubble," and that is a good metaphor that is easy for students to remember. We are trapped in a "filter bubble" and not exposed to information that can challenge or broaden our view of the world, which in the end will prove to be bad for us and bad for democracy. (Pariser, 2011)

The search engine logic makes it difficult for our students to find relevant and valid sources. According to Alan November (2012), author of the book Who Owns the Learning, one of the essential skills in a student's digital competence today is their ability to validate the information they find online. The International Computer and Information Literacy Study (ICILS) 2013 (Otterstad, 2013) compared secondary school students' digital skills in 18 countries and found that about one-third of middle school students lack necessary digital skills. In other words, they are not able to navigate safely in our digital information society. What makes it more complicated is that students, when asked, have great faith in their abilities to search for information. According to the ICILS study in 2013, 79% of Norwegian students say they can assess whether they can rely on information they find on the web. Almost as many say that they have learned these skills on their own (Otterstad, 2013). In other words, most students do not learn about this in school. This supports the theory of Alan November that students have a great deal of confidence in their abilities when it comes to searching the web but that those skills are vastly overrated.

> These days, the world is also online. Technology facilitates political participation and contributes to keeping us informed – or not. As social media develops, people increasingly rely on online information that is shared by those they trust. But such information is not always verifiable, which can make it difficult to sort fact from fiction. This challenges our capacity to make informed decisions and undermines the quality of public deliberations.
>
> (OECD, 2017)

Schools need to provide their students with the civic and political knowledge required for adult life. "In the 21st century, this requires a focus on digital democratic citizenship and the kind of skills and attitudes that come with it. Sustaining democratic institutions and social relations over time depends on the way we support and encourage young people to become active and engaged citizens, both on and offline" (Fuster, 2017).

A good rule for finding out if a source is reliable is to cross-check other sources when you perform a search. "Trust but verify" is a Russian proverb that former president Ronald Reagan frequently used. The first results are often on top because someone paid for them to be on top. If you look farther down the list and they all have the same claim, then you have verified your conclusions. My advice is to use more than two sources. Teach students how to investigate who is the author of a website and why they wrote that particular article. Newsguard (2020) is a service that identifies sources and tells whether they are trustworthy: "NewsGuard uses journalism to fight false news, misinformation, and disinformation. Our trained analysts, who are experienced journalists, research online news brands to help readers and viewers know which ones are trying to do legitimate journalism – and which are not."

You can download it as an extension for Safari or Chrome and when you search you will see a green rating icon that verifies that it is trustworthy (see Figure 8.3).

Classroom application

Here are some websites that are designed to fool us. Have students review them and then discuss the intentions of those who created these pages:

1. GenoChoice – Create your own genetically healthy child
2. Dog Island – A vacation spot for dogs where they can play and have fun
3. Mankato, Minnesota – A delightful holiday paradise where temperatures are constant 21 degrees Celsius

When searching for information, how many sources do you use? How do you distinguish false news from factual information? Why is it seemingly so hard to identify? Many articles may contain both incorrect and honest information. Often, the concept of false or fake news can be misleading because there can be a mix of truth and misinformation in the articles we find. That is why it is so important to verify by reading multiple sources. It is also a fact that so-called false/fake news spreads faster because we are often tempted to share something that seems absurd and provocative. Fake news plays on feelings and prejudice. When we have a strong passion for a cause, we quickly become less critical. Therefore, the chances of sharing the material increases. Always ask yourself, "Is it a little too unbelievable to be true?" Because if the answer is yes, then it may be just that. Are you able to find this news somewhere else? Check before you share. Sharing fake news is a danger to democracy. Why it is, is a topic to discuss with your class.

Planning time spent online

Initially, I mentioned that being able to find reliable sources is an integral part of our digital judgment. Teachers are great at assessing relevant information that students

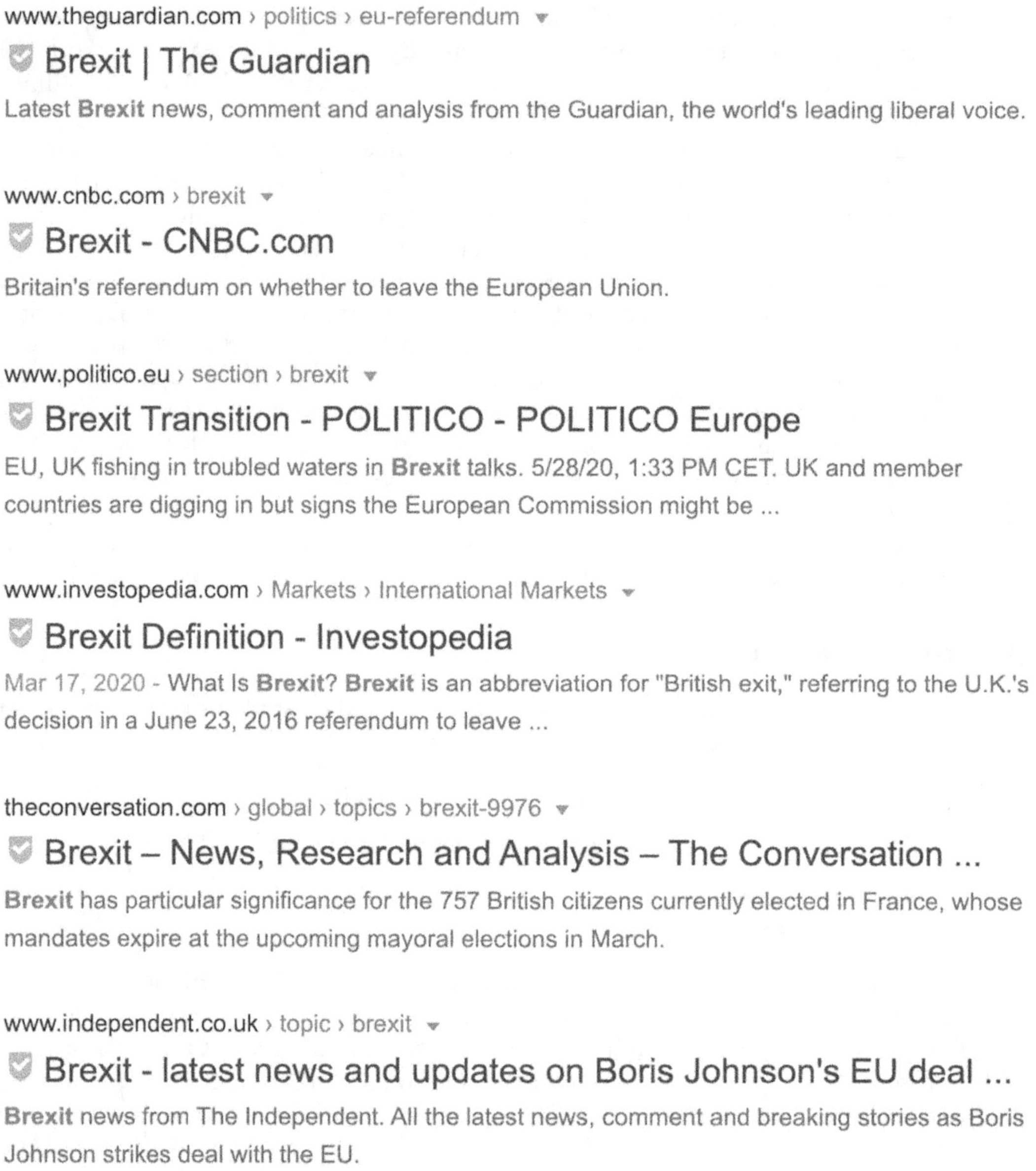

www.theguardian.com › politics › eu-referendum ▼
Brexit | The Guardian
Latest **Brexit** news, comment and analysis from the Guardian, the world's leading liberal voice.

www.cnbc.com › brexit ▼
Brexit - CNBC.com
Britain's referendum on whether to leave the European Union.

www.politico.eu › section › brexit ▼
Brexit Transition - POLITICO - POLITICO Europe
EU, UK fishing in troubled waters in **Brexit** talks. 5/28/20, 1:33 PM CET. UK and member countries are digging in but signs the European Commission might be ...

www.investopedia.com › Markets › International Markets ▼
Brexit Definition - Investopedia
Mar 17, 2020 - What Is **Brexit**? **Brexit** is an abbreviation for "British exit," referring to the U.K.'s decision in a June 23, 2016 referendum to leave ...

theconversation.com › global › topics › brexit-9976 ▼
Brexit – News, Research and Analysis – The Conversation ...
Brexit has particular significance for the 757 British citizens currently elected in France, whose mandates expire at the upcoming mayoral elections in March.

www.independent.co.uk › topic › brexit ▼
Brexit - latest news and updates on Boris Johnson's EU deal ...
Brexit news from The Independent. All the latest news, comment and breaking stories as Boris Johnson strikes deal with the EU.

FIGURE 8.3 Results from the search "Brexit".

need in their learning, and they can help their learners use material found online. What is not so obvious perhaps is that we should also teach our students how to control the time spent online and which resources to use to understand the material they are studying. When is it smart to use digital tools? Discuss with your students how they prepare for tests and how they do homework. Are they easily distracted by messages popping up on their screen all the time? And how about yourself? How effectively do you work when planning or correcting papers online? Are you tempted to look up topics online, and are you easily carried away?

In my class, I have deliberately engaged students in testing different ways of learning with and without digital tools. Students have taken notes using shared documents in Google and OneNote and compared it with the use of paper and pencil. We have closed the internet, put away phones, and worked in groups with only one PC. Since the internet is mostly open – websites are not closed in Norway – it makes for some interesting conversations. What if a student is watching Netflix movies all day? All teachers should ask their students these questions: How do you learn best? Which method works best for you, for the class, for this particular curriculum goal, and for this topic? It is an exciting journey, for this is uncharted territory for some, with no easy answers. Another important aspect here is to take many different ways toward the goal of mastery. Today, we should be able to tailor learning to suit every student. Using digital learning tools can help us.

An important point in such a discussion is time planning and attention management. In his book *The Shallows: What the Internet Is Doing to Our Brains*, research journalist Nicholas Carr (2010) asks the question, "Is Google making us stupid?" Carr describes numerous scientific studies that lend support to his claim that web surfing has adverse cognitive consequences. For example, research has shown that readers of hypertext have more difficulty understanding and remembering what they have read than do readers of traditional, "linear" text. In multiple studies, the distraction of hyperlinks was shown to hinder comprehension (Carr, 2010). He points out that several studies have found that reading online encourages quick, distracted, and superficial reading. There's nothing wrong with absorbing information quickly and in bits and pieces. We've always skimmed newspapers more than we've read them, and we routinely run our eyes over books and magazines to get the gist of a piece of writing and decide whether it warrants more thorough reading. The ability to scan and browse is as important as the ability to read deeply and think attentively. What's disturbing is that skimming is becoming our dominant mode of thought. Once a means to an end, a way to identify information for further study, it's becoming an end in itself – our preferred method of both learning and analyzing. Dazzled by the internet's treasures, we have been blind to the damage we may be doing to our intellectual lives and even our culture (Carr, 2010).

We are easily distracted by messages popping up on the screen. However, "push" notifications can be controlled, and it is possible to make the digital environment more learning-friendly. Discuss with your class if you can agree on a common strategy.

The Pomodoro Technique

I have already discussed deeper learning and how it aligns with how students learn, with the use of digital tools. It is, however, essential to watch out for distractions, the so-called time thieves, as students sit down to work on assignments and prepare for assessments. At my school, we have worked with a technique called the Pomodoro Technique (Cirillo, 2018) with our students. It has proved to be a smart way for students to work without distractions. The tomato timer is how Francesco Cirillo got inspired to invent the time management system known as the Pomodoro Technique. You can download the Pomodoro software from Cirillo's website, for free, or you can go to the Tomato Timer web app from any browser and use it instantly, occasionally, or bookmark it for daily use (Cirillo, 2018).

I used and tested several of the following apps when I was writing this book. Be aware that some of these are paid services.

POPULAR POMODORO APPS

Focus booster: Simple Pomodoro timer. Focus booster is a free desktop app that aims to help improve your focus and productivity.

PomoDone: a Chrome extension that allows you to create tasks right from the browser (Mac & Win version only)

Forest: an app that is also an extension to Google Chrome. The idea is that you plant a seed in the forest. In the next 30 minutes, it will grow into a tree. However, if you cannot resist the temptation and start to browse the tree will wither away.

Toggl: a time tracking app operated by Toggl OÜ, headquartered in Tallinn, Estonia, that offers online time tracking and reporting services through its website along with mobile and desktop applications

POPULAR APPS TO BLOCK DISTRACTING WEBSITES

Freedom: if you need to focus on your work, break a habit, or simply improve your relationship with technology, Freedom can help. By blocking distracting websites and apps, you'll be more focused and productive.

StayFocused: a productivity extension for Google Chrome that helps you stay focused on work by restricting the amount of time you can spend on time-wasting websites. Once your allotted time has been used up, the sites you have blocked will be inaccessible for the rest of the day.

Self-control: a free and open-source application for MacOS that lets you block your access to distracting websites, your mail servers, or anything else on the internet. Just set a time to block for, add sites to your blacklist, and click "Start." Until that timer expires, you will be unable to access those sites – even if you restart your computer or delete the application.

FocalFilter: a free productivity tool that helps you focus by temporarily blocking distracting websites. After the block timer runs out, your websites are available for you to view again.

POPULAR APPS FOR BACKGROUND NOISE

A study in the *Journal of Consumer Research* (Ravi Mehta, 2012) shows that background noise as mundane as the hum of a coffee shop in full swing or the muffled chatter of television in the other room can enhance performance. There are many apps for this:

Noisli: a free app that you need to register that offers a choice between Productivity, Random, and Relax. An upgrade is required for Noise Blocker and Motivation. It has a timer for the 25 minutes you have set for working concentrated.

Classroom application

Go through the following list with your class and explain why these items are important. Have the students test this out at home in preparation for a test.

- Make a list of topics you need to study.
- Prioritize your list of topics by due date and importance.
- Gather material you need to study, including a timer. You can use a kitchen timer or your phone.
- Turn off all distractions, including putting your phone on "Do Not Disturb," and turning off notifications on your computer.
- Set a timer for 25 minutes.
- Work on the task until the timer expires.
- Take a short break (5 minutes).
- Every four "**Pomodoro**," take a long break (10 minutes) and a little reward for good work. Repeat if you need more time.

It is important teachers discuss with their students which digital tools to use and when. Without careful consideration, teachers and students might forget why they are using a particular tool and lose sight of their ultimate goal: improving student learning and understanding. The extent to which teachers and their students view educational technology as a tool rather than as the target will shape how technology is used in the classroom.

When it comes to digital tools in education, it is best not to think to start with the tools but with the pedagogy. It is like professor Marte Blikstad-Balas describes in Chapter 10:

> In fact, a key take-home message from educational research is that digital tools – including devices like smartboards, tablets, computers, or mobile phones and software like PowerPoint, Google Docs, or Kahoot – are less important for students' learning than the ways teachers are able to use these tools across subjects.
> (p. 112)

Think about what approach would be the best to help your students learn, and then look for tools that facilitate that approach. The focus should always be the students, not the teacher.

A digital tool can help you reach the goal faster and, and when used correctly, can help students in their learning. Goodhart's law is expressed simply as "When a measure becomes a target, it ceases to be a good measure". I guess you can say the same for digital tools.

We must acknowledge that everyone learns differently and that we have different levels of coping with distractions and self-discipline regarding work ethics. There is not a one-size-fits-all aspect here, and we need to adjust accordingly. This is an ongoing challenge.

Using technology to save the world

There are areas where we have the opportunity to do a little better. One of those areas is how we teach digital citizenship. Most teachers will say that this is taught in their school, but where we seem to disagree is in how we do this. It is easy to confuse digital citizenship with online safety. Because digital citizenship is about making your community better, to engage with people who have different views and beliefs respectfully, online safety is something else: to be able to shape and change public policy and to be able to recognize the validity of online sources of information.

Digital citizenship, and here is the catch, has to be taught in context. It is challenging for students to learn something out of context. How many times have you talked to your students about how we should look out for each other just to see that they do not think about how this applies to students in their class. If we don't teach students how to use social media to make a difference and if we don't teach students how to organize people around a good cause, we should not be surprised if they only use their devices for entertainment. If we want our students to understand how to use technology to improve their community to amplify their voice and how to distinguish fact from fiction online, we have to teach those skills in a virtual space.

Digital citizenship, it turns out, is not a list of don'ts but a list of dos. And never has it been more critical to address this than it is now.

Learning how to be a caring digital citizen is not something that happens if we don't actively teach it. And preparing a generation of digital citizens is the most important thing we can do to ensure democracy for the future.

References

Carr, N. (2010). *The shallows: What the internet is doing to our brains.* New Yor, NY: W.W. Norton & Company.
Cirillo, F. (2018). *The Pomodoro Technique: The life-changing time-management system.* London: Ebury Publishing.
Fuster, M. (2017, December 15). *Citizenship and education in a digital world.* From OECD Education and Skills Today: https://oecdedutoday.com/citizenship-and-education-in-a-digital-world/
Google. (2020, June 3). *Be internet awesome.* From Digital Safety Resources: https://beinternetawesome.withgoogle.com/en_us/educators
NewsGuard. (2020, June 3). *NewsGuard.* From The Internet Trust Tool: https://www.newsguardtech.com/
November, A. (2012). *Who owns the learning: Preparing the students for success in the digital age.* Bloomington, IN: Solution Tree.
Organisation for Economic Co-operation and Development. (2017, December 15). *Citizenship and education in a digital world.* From OECD Education and Skills Today: https://oecdedutoday.com/citizenship-and-education-in-a-digital-world/
Organisation for Economic Co-operation and Development. (2018). *OECD future of education and skills: 2030 project background.* Paris: Author.
Otterstad, T. (2013). *Digitale ferdigheter for alle? Norske resultater fra ICILS.* Oslo: Universitetet i Oslo.
Pariser, E. (2011). *The filter bubble: What the internet is hiding from you.* New York, NY: Penguin Press.
Ravi Mehta, R. Z. (2012). Is noise always bad? Exploring the effects of ambien noise on creative cognition. *Journal of Consumer Research,* V(i), 784–799.
Rheingold, H. (2012). *Net smart: How to thrive online.* Cambridge, MA: The MIT Press.

CHAPTER 9

Special needs education

Ann S. Michaelsen

Introduction

This book provides a wide range of examples of how to use digital technologies to enhance students' learning. Most of the tools and classroom applications can easily be used in any classroom with every student. The reason I chose to write a separate chapter for special needs students is that it is a common misconception among educators that technology should not be used with students who are struggling to learn. In Norway, it is compulsory to customize teaching to facilitate every student, especially those with learning disabilities. In my opinion, we now have many tools that can help us here. It is a lot easier if we know what is available, how to use it, and when. In this chapter, I show some examples of what we can do for students who have specific challenges in school, with an emphasis on software that helps students with reading and writing and the use of virtual reality (VR) technology, which offers many apps and games to learn.

Software that helps students read and write

Dyslexia is a learning disorder that involves difficulty reading due to problems identifying speech sounds and learning how they relate to letters and words (decoding). Also called reading disability, dyslexia affects areas of the brain that process language. People with dyslexia have normal intelligence and usually have normal vision. Most children with dyslexia can succeed in school with tutoring or a specialized education program (Mayo Clinic, 2019).

My claim is that all children can succeed in school if they have teachers who can navigate in this complex and overwhelming myriad of software and technology. And it is our job as educators to find suitable alternatives for these students so that their difficulties with reading and writing do not become an obstacle in their learning. Students can listen to the material, discuss with classmates, watch, talk about, and experience. Instead of writing, they can dictate, they can use audio, video, and film for their performances and presentations.

As mentioned earlier, the teacher's digital competence largely determines how students use technology when learning. It is important to stress that every school has to be sure that the teachers have the proper training to work like this. It is unfortunate if some students get guidance in this area when others do not. Therefore, every teacher should have knowledge about technological solutions and software that can help this group of students. This is an area that needs improvement. See Chapter 10, "The Digital Classroom: What Is the Insight From Contemporary Educational Research?" where professor Marte Blikstad-Balaas points to studies that support this claim. She points to research that finds student teachers and novice teachers tend to report that they do not feel that their teacher education has prepared them for the use of digital technology in their classrooms.

Some students may only need to learn how to use the advanced features of software like Microsoft Word, to provide the tools they need to communicate effectively.

In a three case studies of dyslexic writers in higher education, Price (2006) found that the use of different types of software could overcome writing anxiety, "fear of the blank page" syndrome and issues of plagiarism:

> The Vygotskian model for the development of gradual student control relies upon the notion of students working alongside an expert who can guide them in managing their own learning environment. This has implications for both assessment of need and specialist tutorial support. The experiences of the students within the case studies demonstrate that often simple software can provide the best solutions, and that students combine features from software programs in creative ways to compensate for weaknesses in their cognitive profile.

There are many programs made for special education. If you are lucky, your school has already bought those for you. In this chapter, I share functionalities in software you might already be using and therefore is familiar to you and the students. Like the dictation opportunities that are included in both Microsoft products and Google Docs. After dictating, it can be a good idea to use the function "*Read Aloud*" to be sure the dictation program got it right.

Students with dyslexia often have difficulty writing words correctly. Many programs can help students here, both with writing support and dictation opportunities. When dictating, the students do not have to write themselves. They can dictate the text, and the speech recognition program translates it into writing. This can be a great help for many students, not only those who have dyslexia. It can also be useful in language learning (see Figure 9.1). You find the tool for dictate on the right side of the window in Microsoft Word.

Word prediction uses text suggestions to help you find the right way to spell difficult words. When you start typing the first letters in the word, the program predicts the word and shows you alternatives you can choose. The words appear from a list, and the students choose the word from that list. This means that you can enter words that are often mistyped and that the program suggests the correct spelling. To use this in Microsoft Word, you need to change settings in Windows. Choose "*Devices, typing,*"

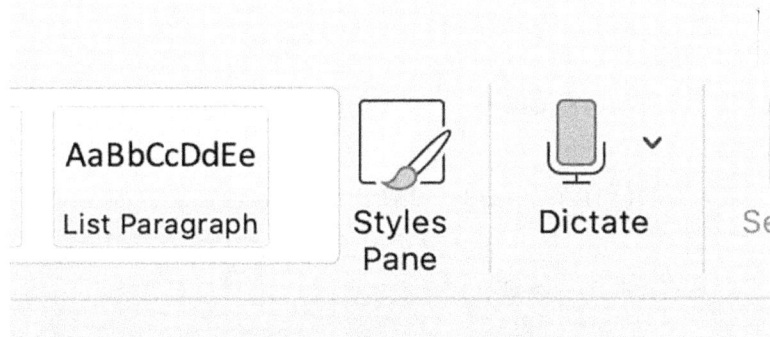

FIGURE 9.1 This is how using Microsoft Word for dictation looks.

FIGURE 9.2 This is what Read Aloud looks like.

and toggle on "*Spelling, Typing, and Hardware Keyboard.*" Google Chrome and Google Docs have the same functionality.

There is also a nice thesaurus feature in Microsoft Word. You can find it in the "*Tools*" menu. Select it and get an entire list of suggestions on the right side as you type. This can be a help for all learners to improve their language. In Google, they have many similar options that let you search for synonyms. First, you have to install the add-on in your browser.

You can also use the function "*Read Aloud*" to get your text read aloud. You can get your own text or a text from the web read aloud for you. Put the cursor where you want the reading to begin, then press Play, and adjust the speed to the desired rate. It can be an excellent way for the student to hear that what they have written is correct, so this feature is a useful support for students with reading and writing difficulties. It may also be applicable in foreign languages. This is available both in Microsoft Word and in Google Docs. In Google, you can choose the add-on as a Chrome Extension, or you can go through the menu "*Accessibility*" (Figure 9.2).

← The House intelligence committee chairman, Adam Schiff, c...

The House in·tel·li·gence com·mit·tee chair·man, Ad·am Schiff, called the com·ments "de·tes·ta·ble". On Fri·day, Warm·bier's par·ents blamed Kim's " e·vil re·gime" for his death and said: "No ex·cuse of

FIGURE 9.3 This is what Immersive Reader looks like with color-coded nouns, verbs, and adjectives.

Immersive Reader, included in OneNote Learning Tools, is a full-screen reading experience to increase the readability of content in OneNote documents. The tools are designed to support students with dyslexia and dysgraphia (inability to write coherently as a symptom of brain disease or damage) in the classroom but can assist anyone who wants to make reading on their device easier. It enables students with dyslexia to use text decoding solutions and helps build confidence. You can enable learners regardless of age or ability with easy to use features that reduce visual crowding, highlight text, break words into syllables, read text aloud, and provide visual references (Figure 9.3).

For the younger students, I recommend the Picture Dictionary capability built directly into the Immersive Reader. Have the text read up for you, click on the word, and have a single word read out, and if it is a noun, you might see a picture. The ability to see a picture and see and hear the word simultaneously (multisensory processing) is a technique to aid reading and comprehension. With the Picture Dictionary, a student can click on a word and immediately see a related picture and have the ability to use the "*Read Aloud*" as many times as necessary (Figure 9.4).

If all teachers were aware of the dictation and reading functions and used them actively in class, many students who now struggle to write correctly and understand texts would be able to experience mastery in areas where they previously have been struggling.

FIGURE 9.4 Picture Dictionary with the picture of a pond.

Searching for information

As described in Chapter 8 searching for information can be difficult and once students are searching online, they might lose track of time. Keeping students focused on the document they are writing is always a goal. Therefore, it is a good idea to know that you can search for information while you are writing your text.

When your students are searching for information, why not use the different tools directly in Word. In the Tools menu, you find not only the Thesaurus but also Smart Lookup, Researcher, and Translate. These are very useful functions, and at the same time, remind students to include information about the sources they use. Just right-click on a word or highlight a group of words and right-click them, and from the menu, select Smart Lookup. Smart Lookup uses the context around the word, not only the words themselves, to give you more relevant results (see Figure 9.5). You get a new menu on the right of your text divided in "*Explore*" and "*Define*" (see Figure 9.6). "*Explore*" uses a Bing search a web search and an explore Wikipedia search. The "*Define*" tab uses the Oxford Dictionaries from Oxford University Press. You can also instantly translate texts you are working on. Just highlight the text and right click and choose to translate. Researcher gives you journals and websites with research on a topic you are interested in. It is useful when students are writing papers.

VR glasses in class

The use of VR glasses is relatively new in school, but if you Google VR glasses in education, you will see that a growing number of schools have taken it into use. VR is short for "virtual reality." It is an illusion generated using different types of technology (three-dimensional [3D] images and sound) that gives the user an experience of being located in a different place, real or fictional. It provides opportunities for students to experience a world that is otherwise inaccessible, like a visit to a museum far way or

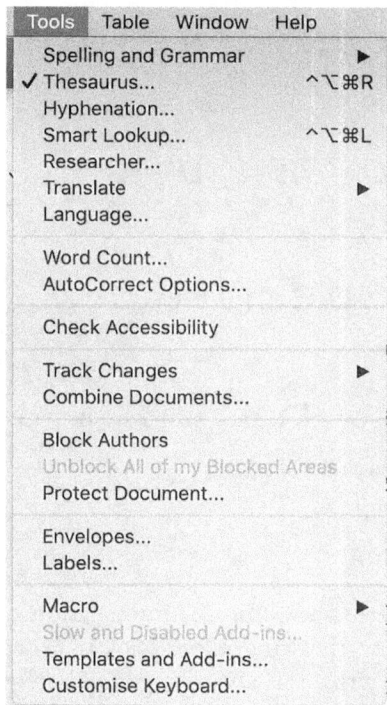

FIGURE 9.5 Look under the menu "*Tools*" for Thesaurus, Smart Lookup, and Researcher.

a dive into the human body. Everyone with vision can participate regardless of their disabilities.

A study (Allcoat & von Mulenen, 2018) in the use of VR in which 99 participants were assigned to one of three learning conditions – traditional (textbook-style), VR, and video (a passive control) – found that those who used VR showed better performance. The learning materials used the same text and 3D model for all conditions. Each participant was given a knowledge test before and after learning. Participants in the traditional and VR conditions had improved overall performance (i.e., learning, including knowledge acquisition and understanding) compared to those in the video condition. Participants in the VR condition also showed better performance for "remembering" than those in the traditional and video conditions. Emotion self-ratings before and after the learning phase showed an increase in positive emotions and a decrease in negative emotions for the VR condition. Conversely, there was a decrease in positive emotions in both the traditional and video conditions. The web-based learning tools evaluation scale also found that participants in the VR condition reported higher engagement than those in the other conditions. Overall, VR displayed an improved learning experience when compared to traditional and video learning methods (Allcoat & von Mulenen, 2018).

Virtual reality opens up new opportunities in teaching but is still at an early stage. Most of the software is used for entertainment. The challenge is to find programs that

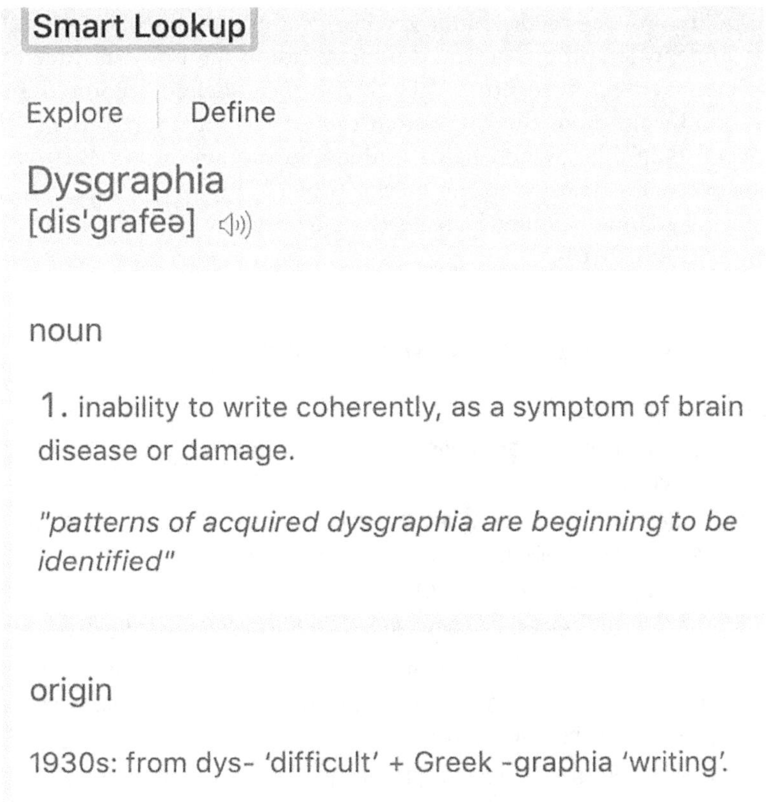

> **Smart Lookup**
>
> Explore | Define
>
> # Dysgraphia
> [dis'grafēə] 🔊
>
> noun
>
> 1. inability to write coherently, as a symptom of brain disease or damage.
>
> *"patterns of acquired dysgraphia are beginning to be identified"*
>
> origin
>
> 1930s: from dys- 'difficult' + Greek -graphia 'writing'.

FIGURE 9.6 Smart Lookup gives you the definitions of words right in the document you are writing in.

build up under the various subjects' curriculum goals. The technology can be used to motivate and encourage student participation and to create shared experiences that are accessible to everyone.

Video and images in VR provide visual support and helps actualize lessons, a way to explain theoretical themes that are hard to grasp. Like understanding how different organs in the body function, exploring the inside of the body to see the different angles and functions of the organ can make it more tangible and visual. If you think lab work is challenging, working with VR glasses can make it easier to see the effects of what you do on a cellular or molecular level.

This opportunity to learn through being in the center and with hands-on experience makes it easier to learn and remember, as opposed to looking at pictures in a book and reading a text, with many opportunities for conceptual learning and language stimulation. As an example, the Expeditions app can be used both to give students an experience of the Northern Lights and to help them work on conceptual learning and language understanding: Students can describe what they see, location, positions, characteristics, phenomena, functions, and experiences. VR can be a great motivator and is used in many higher educational institutions. VR is a good solution for highly technical training fields like the military or the medical industry. For example, the most significant challenge for medical students learning anatomy is understanding the body in three dimensions and how different systems fit together. VR education can help overcome this problem.

One good example is the VR system used by Mendel Grammar School in Opava City, Czech Republic, which helps students in biology classes learn about the anatomy of the eye. The team working on this project employed a Leap Motion controller and specially adapted Oculus Rift headsets to provide an innovative way of learning anatomy (Babich, 2019).

> **EXAMPLES OF APPS AND GAMES FOR SCHOOL USE**
>
> Boulevard: Walk around museums from all over the world. http://blvrd.com/
>
> Apollo 11 VR: Learn lessons about the Apollo 11/lunar landing. https://immersivevreducation.com/products-vr-experiences/apollo-11/
>
> Sites in VR: Go around and look at landmarks from around the world. https://play.google.com/store/apps/details?id=air.com.ercangigi.sitesin3d
>
> School Fab Lab VR: Technology like 3D printers, CNC machines, drones, and much more. https://store.steampowered.com/app/827280/School_Fab_Lab_VR/
>
> VictoryVR: All science (created specifically for American students). https://www.victoryvr.biz/
>
> BBC Earth: Life in VR: Swim around with life in the sea. https://play.google.com/store/apps/details?id=com.bbc.lifeinvr01&hl=en_US
>
> Expeditions: Expeditions to landmarks, mountain peaks, space, and more. https://play.google.com/store/apps/details?id=com.google.vr.expeditions&hl=en_US
>
> Unimersiv: A bit of everything, dinosaurs, anatomy, space, ancient landmarks, and much more. https://unimersiv.com/

I would recommend searching for apps and games in VR within the subject you want to cover in school, as well as in the technology you use. Keep in mind that almost no games or apps work for all VR devices, and it's important to carefully review the technical requirements of the game or app before purchasing a system.

VR and augmented reality (AR) are often used equally interchangeably, especially for smartphones. VR is about replacing as many sensory impressions as possible with virtual digital impressions. The 3D effect is central to VR. There are also the audio impressions you get through headphones. Here, a layer of additional digital content is added on top of an image. This can be used, for example, to plan furniture in a room. At high schools in Norway, they use this for design and architecture, where students use it in urban planning.

You might have heard about all three: VR, AR, and mixed reality. Many confuse the difference between these. VR is probably the most well-known technology. You might have your own VR set at home for games. When used your brain believes you are moving among virtual objects on a screen. You can use a head-mounted display or a VR headset. The headset is often connected to a PC or console that enables the virtual experience. I'm sure you have heard about how surgeons plan surgery with this technology. It is also used to visit a travel destination even before they take flight. It can also be used by children to walk on the moon and soldiers train for combat scenarios.

Augmented reality rather than provide a fully immersive virtual experience, enhance the real-world with images, text, and other virtual information via devices such as heads-up displays, smartphones, tablets, smart lenses, and AR glasses. Imagine being on a self-guided walking tour and wanting to know details about the architecture of a building you discover. With an augmented reality technology app, you could just point your phone at the building, and all the details are projected in your line of sight. A mixed-reality environment goes a step beyond augmented reality because users can interact in real-time with virtual objects that are placed within the real world. These virtual items will respond and react to users as if they were actual objects.

(Marr, 2019)

References

Allcoat, D. A., & von Mulenen, A. (2018). *Learning in virtual reality: Effects on performance, emotion and engagement*. Coventry, England: Research in Learning Technology.

Babich, N. (2019, September 19). *How VR In education will change how we learn and teach*. From Adobe: https://xd.adobe.com/ideas/principles/emerging-technology/virtual-reality-will-change-learn-teach/

Marr, B. (2019, July 19). *The important difference between virtual reality, augmented reality and mixed reality*. From *Forbes*: https://www.forbes.com/sites/bernardmarr/2019/07/19/the-important-difference-between-virtual-reality-augmented-reality-and-mixed-reality/#604a7d2835d3

Mayo Clinic. (2019, July 2). *Dyslexia*. From Drugs.com know more be sure: https://www.drugs.com/mcd/dyslexia

Price, G. A. (2006). Creative solutions to making the technology work. *Research in Learning Technology*, 14(1), 21–38.

CHAPTER 10

The digital classroom
What is the insight from contemporary educational research?

Marte Blikstad-Balas

Digital technology in the classroom – yay or nay?

Many educational politicians, researchers, and practitioners around the world consider digital competence to be a crucial aspect of education, which schools should systematically develop (Ferrari, 2013; Griffin, Care, & McGaw, 2012). There is a general consensus that students will need to have extensive digital competence to meet the demands of any future job. There is also a general agreement about the rather obvious fact that digital technology is everywhere in the Western world and that students are used to having access to such technologies in every aspect of their lives (Dunn, Gray, Moffett, & Mitchell, 2018; Howard, Yang, Ma, Maton, & Rennie, 2018). Despite such consensus, the topic of how schools should integrate technology in their everyday instruction is still hotly debated. Questions that are guaranteed to cause debate in almost any social setting include the following: Should children in the first grade get their own tablet for school purposes? How much screen time is acceptable during the school day? Will students learn more or better by using digital technology? While some people have strong opinions about the problems and possible dangers of introducing digital technologies in schools, others are equally convinced about all the benefits of making learning more digital. Thus, debates about technology tend to become very polarized. Both sides in debates about the merits of technology in school can find solid empirical evidence to support their claims, as research has highlighted a range of benefits and problems when increasing students' access to digital technologies in the classroom.

The benefits of drawing on digital technology for students are documented through ample research. Studies have repeatedly found that students enjoy using technology and that use of technology outside of school can have positive impacts on school performance. For example, Brevik (2016) showed how a group of Norwegian high school students scored significantly higher on reading proficiency in English than in their mother tongue, Norwegian, due, in part, to the number of video games and video game–related interactions in English these students engaged in. Furthermore, O'Brien, Beach, and Scharber (2007) found that students' experience with video games can benefit them in their reading and writing at school because they can draw on their experiences with narrative structures from various complex video games. Kucirkova and Sakr (2015) found that the use of tablets can enhance children's creative expression, and Flewitt, Messer, and Kucirkova (2015) showed how tablets can offer rich opportunities for children to engage in collaborative interaction and independent learning. In addition to these studies, research has documented the benefits of specific apps, games, and devices for education. For example, Silseth (2012) investigated how educators used the game Global Conflicts: Palestine when teaching students about the Israel–Palestine conflict, while Siew, Geofrey, and Lee (2016) found that students who learned algebra using the app DragonBox 12+ showed significantly higher mean scores in algebraic thinking and attitudes toward algebra compared to the control group who did not use the app. Hennessy and London (2013) explored how different digital affordances available through interactive whiteboards can help students to express their ideas about content knowledge. These are just some examples, but they all show how digital technology can play a key role in learning inside and outside of school.

In contrast to the positive findings of the role of digital technology described so far, a number of studies have also shed light on the more problematic aspects of providing students with more access to digital technologies. For instance, some studies have documented how high school students who have access to the internet during the school day may spend a significant amount of time in class, during teacher instruction, engaging in social media, reading blogs, and playing games through their laptops or their smartphones (Blikstad-Balas, 2012; Elstad, 2006; Sahlström, Tanner, & Valasmo, 2019). Evidence has also suggested that students who spend time on nonacademic content on their laptops tend to distract their peers and hinder not just their own learning but also the learning of others (Sana, Weston, & Cepeda, 2013). Furthermore, studies have challenged the notion that digital is always better. For example, studies on reading have repeatedly shown how reading on paper is superior to the screen when it comes to reading comprehension (Delgado, Vargas, Ackerman, & Salmerón, 2018; Støle, Mangen, & Schwippert, 2020).

The myth about a generation of so-called digital natives has also been seriously challenged by a multitude of studies showing how young people use (and refrain from using) digital technologies in a number of different ways and acquire different levels of digital competence (Michelsen, 2015; Westlund & Bjur, 2014). Several studies have also attempted to measure and link the access and use of digital technology at the classroom or student level to measurable learning outcomes. This approach has been used by several large-scale surveys and assessment studies, for example, by the Organisation for Economic Co-operation and Development (OECD) Programme for International Student Assessment (PISA) tests and secondary analyses of PISA data. These studies have not found any evince that access to digital technology will increase learning in any way. Over the last 10 years, researchers have found no improvement in student achievement in reading, science, or mathematics that can be related to a massive investment in digitalization of the classroom (e.g., Claro et al., 2012; Díaz et al., 2019; OECD, 2015).

As this very brief review suggests, many solid studies support "both sides" of the debate on whether the adoption of technology in schools is beneficial or harmful. To make the picture even more complex, a large body of research on the effectiveness of utilizing digital technologies in school has produced mixed results. For example, a study comparing preschooler reading of eBooks on tablets with traditional print books (Reich, Yau, & Warschauer, 2016) found that children learned equally well when reading a well-designed eBook and sometimes even more than when reading the print book. However, Reich et al. (2016) also found that enhancements such as sounds, animations, and games could reduce learning through eBooks because they distracted children. Furthermore, Reich et al. (2016) also found that when children were sharing a traditional print book with an adult, the conversation would often revolve around the book content, but during eBook reading, the conversation would often be around the platform.

It may seem confusing that researchers and studies point to a number of positive, negative, and mixed results of technology use. There is an easy explanation: The question of whether or not to include technology in education is far too simplistic. The complexity of teaching and learning cannot be reduced to a question of digital or traditional affordances, regardless of the social contexts in which technology is embedded. This latter point also has substantial research to support it. In fact, a key take-home message from educational research is that digital tools – including devices like smartboards, tablets, computers, or mobile phones and software like PowerPoint, Google Docs, or Kahoot – are less important for students' learning than the ways teachers are able to use these tools across subjects (Baker, Goodboy, Bowman, & Wright, 2018; Blikstad-Balas & Davies, 2017; Jewitt, Moss, & Cardini, 2007; Lei & Zhao, 2007). Successful uptake of technology in an educational context is not a one-size-fits-all effort, and several factors always come into play. In the following section, we will look into some of these factors that have been identified as important when implementing digital technology in the classroom: access to relevant hardware and software, teachers' competence, and teachers' attitude towards teaching with *digital technology*.

Access to relevant hardware and software

Digital technology infrastructure is an obvious prerequisite for integrating digital technology into instruction in meaningful ways. At the school level, the inadequacy of such structures can be a key barrier to Information and communications technology implementation (Baydas & Goktas, 2016; Bingimlas, 2009; Gil-Flores, Rodríguez-Santero, & Torres-Gordillo, 2017). In many countries, the question of access has dominated the discourse around digital technology implementation for decades, and many school districts report pressure to provide 1:1 access – one device for each student (Blikstad-Balas & Davies, 2017). However, it is important to remember that access alone is not a reliable predictor of teachers' actual implementation of digital technology (Gil-Flores et al., 2017). There is a crucial difference between providing access and preparing teachers to actually utilize the technology they get access to in their everyday teaching.

Norway is an interesting case when it comes to the differences between having the digital infrastructure and utilizing this infrastructure well. The country has been a front runner in providing schools with digital technology. The overall access to technology has been consistently high and significantly above the European average for the student-per-laptop ratio (OECD, 2015). Since 2006, digital technology has been defined as a core competence in the Norwegian curriculum, and it has, therefore, also been a priority of the national research agenda to investigate technology uptake (Erstad, 2006; Gudmundsdottir & Hatlevik, 2018). While 1:1 access is the norm in Norwegian upper secondary schools, most lower secondary schools can also provide permanent 1:1 access, lend students laptops or tablets for use in a specific lesson, or take students to a computer room at the school. However, while the broad access to digital technology in Norwegian schools enables broad use of digital technology in the classroom, research has shown that the uptake of this technology is quite limited. Such uptake often revolves around individual tasks and teachers using presentation tools like PowerPoint in quite traditional ways (Blikstad-Balas & Klette, 2020; Klette et al., 2018).

Teachers' competence

Another key factor for the successful implementation of digital technology is teachers' competence. Across countries, student teachers and novice teachers tend to report that they do not feel that their teacher education has prepared them for the use of digital technology in their classrooms. Røkenes and Krumsvik (2016) summarized research on this matter by noting that it has proved challenging in teacher education to promote the inclusion of digital technology in teaching in ways that move beyond basic digital skills.

While newly educated teachers may have vast experience with digital apps and social media, their experience with digital technology for education is often limited and their repertoire of relevant digital technologies for teaching and learning can best be described as restricted (Sang, Valcke, Van Braak, & Tondeur, 2010; Valtonen et al., 2011). These findings are important because they nuance the assumption that young, newly qualified teachers who spend time on social media and a variety of apps automatically will understand how to implement these technologies as instructional tools in and across different school subjects. These findings are also important because previous research has identified that teachers' need for professional development in how to integrate digital technology is the most significant variable in explaining classroom use of digital technology (Gil-Flores et al., 2017).

Several empirical studies have highlighted the somewhat limited tool-oriented approach to digital technology often found in teacher education as problematic (Haugerud, 2011; Tømte, 2013). In Norway, all students are explicitly expected through the national curriculum to develop digital competence through schooling; however, an analysis of curriculum documents in teacher education from Norway showed that technology use did not have a prominent position in those documents (Instefjord & Munthe, 2016, 2017). The studies determined that few learning goals included the integration of technology in teaching, which suggests that digital competence has limited value in these institutions' perceptions of teaching quality and teacher competence.

Teachers' attitudes toward digital technology

In many countries, the attention to digital competence in the classroom is still a matter of whether each particular teacher considers digital competence to be important. For instance, Drent and Meelissen (2008) found that the integration of digital technology has relied on enthusiastic teachers who procure technology and have ambitions of utilizing more technology in their classrooms. Several studies have shown how teachers' positive attitudes toward digital technology are associated with the use of digital technology in the classroom (Anderson & Maninger, 2007; Baş, Kubiatko, & Sünbül, 2016; Lawrence & Tar, 2018). A study by Player-Koro (2012) found that the attitudes that seem to facilitate teachers' digital technology use in the classroom are not, generally, positive attitudes towards digital technology in education; rather, they are specific, positive attitudes about digital technology in pedagogical work with students and colleagues. Furthermore, Grimalt-Álvaro, Ametller, and Pintó (2019) have identified that teachers' beliefs about the use of 1:1 equipment are consistent with their practices.

It is important to note that, while attitudes influence teachers' willingness to use digital technology in the classroom, teachers also rely on a sufficient repertoire of instructional ways to use digital technology to promote learning. General positive attitudes must be followed up with targeted professional devselopment on how to actually integrate digital technology across topics, lessons, subjects, and learners (Blikstad-Balas & Klette, 2020).

Research-based recommendations: what can teachers do to implement digital technology successfully in their lessons?

Research on digital technology in education can be quite disappointing if we read it with all the rather panegyric promises of more and better learning in mind (Elstad, 2016; Selwyn, 2016). The perhaps most important insight from research on this matter is that successful learning in school always will depend on a range of factors and that the ways technology is used for different purposes can both enable and hinder learning. The final section of this chapter provides concrete advice on what teachers should consider when making choices about what digital technologies to use in their classrooms. It draws on the insights offered by many of the studies reviewed so far in this chapter.

1 Teacher > technology

The first advice may seem rather obvious, but it is something that is very often forgotten in debates about technology. What you do as a teacher is far more important for the students' learning than what technologies you give them access to. What does this mean? It means that how teachers use tablets and apps in their classrooms will determine the learning outcomes, not the tablets and apps themselves. To make good use of any digital tool, teachers must have a clear vision of what the students should learn – not just what they should do (Salomon, 2016). The educational rationale behind the tool is crucial. What should students learn by engaging in, for example, a specific app? Why is this particular app the best choice for this learning process? What competences should students draw on and develop by engaging with the specific app? An important point to be made when it comes to specific learning apps is that teachers should know them well and even model how they can best be used by the students to be able to frame the use well in an educational context. This is essential to ensure that what is learned through, for example, a mathematics game like DragonBox that engages students in algebraic thinking can be "transferred" to more traditional algebra tasks. If not, we will risk students becoming better and better at things within specific apps (Dolonen & Kluge, 2015), which is seldom a broad enough learning goal. Teachers are the ones who make the transition of knowledge visible from one situation to the next and the ones who make – and train their students in making – connections between all the different digital tools. If we want students to be learners across specific apps and platforms, this is essential.

2 Trace the learning process

One of the benefits of using digital tools is that it can enable more insight into students' learning processes, something both Michaelsen and Spurkland (Chapter 4) have highlighted. When explaining how he saw his time in the classroom as time spent looking for evidence that learning has occurred or may occur, Spurkland pinpointed one of the aspects where digital technology really does provide the teacher with a plethora of new possibilities. Digital tools where students should produce something often provide us with opportunities to take part in the process in real-time or even trace back the process afterward. There are examples of this, for instance, when teachers in mathematics use tools that make all the students' screens available to them and give them an entry task for the lesson. This approach allows the teacher to see how each student is solving the task: how they begin, what they actually do, and what they struggle with. This can provide valuable information for the rest of the lesson and enable the teacher to follow up with students who either struggled with the task, need to revise or expand their mathematical strategies, or even need more challenging tasks.

Commonly used tools such as Google Docs, Padlet, Talkwall or even the Track Changes function in Microsoft Word can give teachers a lot of insight into how students are engaging in a task and how they have responded to feedback from you or their peers. This is an underused area of digital technology in education, as research has identified little use of such methods; instead, teachers mostly use digital tools either to present information or to give students individual tasks (Blikstad-Balas & Klette, 2020; Grimalt-Álvaro et al., 2019). For decades, researchers have emphasized that more feedback should be offered during the learning process, rather than solely at the end of students' learning (Black, Harrison, Lee, Marshall, & Wiliam, 2004; Black & Wiliam, 1998, 2009). If digital technology is used wisely, it can provide new ways of obtaining information about how students are working and where they are in their learning process. This information is crucial if we want to provide relevant scaffolding for their learning, not just assess their final products.

3 Increase the cognitive activation in the classroom

The need for students to be actively engaged or challenged during instruction is often referred to as cognitive activation, and it has proved to be a key aspect of instructional quality. Lipowsky et al. (2009) explained how cognitive activation as an instructional practice "encourages students to engage in higher-level thinking and thus to develop an elaborated knowledge base" (p. 529). When assessing the level of cognitive activation enabled by a task or a learning activity in a classroom, critical questions we could ask ourselves are these: What intellectual work are students expected to do in the lesson? Are they asked to do a challenging task that requires critical thinking and making judgments? Are they asked to participate in discussions and provide evidence for their claims? Or, which is too often the case, are they asked to passively listen to a teacher without a particular task other than being quiet and perhaps taking notes? The level of cognitive activation increases when students are challenged, for instance, when they are faced with contradiction, are asked to reflect explicitly on their learning, or are tasked with finding links between new and previous content (Lipowsky et al., 2009). The level of cognitive activation similarly decreases in times when the instruction focuses on the "transmission" of subject-matter knowledge (Wade & Moje, 2000) or when students are asked to restate facts or apply already known knowledge.

This discussion of cognitive activation may seem like general advice, but it is directly linked to digital technology in education because we know from previous research that 1:1 access often reinforces traditional teaching. Put simply, when technology is introduced, often teachers teach with their pre-made presentations in PowerPoint, KeyNote, or Prezi, while students use their tablets and computers to write individually, sustaining traditional formats of classroom discourse in which students are quite passive (Blikstad-Balas & Klette, 2020; Grimalt-Álvaro et al., 2019; Klette et al., 2018; Sahlström et al., 2019). One of the areas where digital technology could really change classroom dynamics is through apps like Padlet or Kahoot that can dramatically increase participation from all students.

Another important aspect of low cognitive activation associated with transmissive pedagogies where teachers talk and students, at best, try to pay attention for long periods is that this approach often does not promote critical thinking, which is a very important competence to develop in a digital world where anyone can publish anything. We know from research that students struggle with critical literacy and finding relevant and credible sources for their schoolwork (Foldvik, 2015; Luke, 2019; Wineburg, 2018). This is perhaps not so surprising as most Western school systems have often systematically used texts to transmit established knowledge that should merely be reproduced. We need to teach our students that, while access to facts has never been more constant, access to knowledge and understanding still requires cognitive engagement and effort. While a student can easily Google what, for example, World War II was about, a Google search alone will never be able to provide that student with deep understanding and knowledge (Gee & Hayes, 2011). To develop knowledge, our students must engage with content and see it in connection with what they already knew. Additionally, they must work critically, talk about the content, and try to make it their own. Historical thinking is not something one can achieve through asking Google questions alone, as suggested by the great title of the equally great book by Sam Wineburg (2018) *Why Learn History (When It's Already on Your Phone)*. Learning something – that is, acquiring knowledge and understanding about something – cannot be achieved by simply locating a large number of online sources and repeating what they say, regardless of how good those sources might be.

4 Connect to the outside world

Several of the chapters in this book are all about connecting the classroom to the so-called outside world, the non-classroom. There are so many good reasons for this, connected to motivation, authenticity, and valuing student experiences. As a literacy researcher, I would like to add another reason that is seldomly discussed. I think a key reason to include texts from a range of authors and perspectives into the classroom is that it will better prepare students for the amount of texts they are bound to meet everywhere outside of school. Textbooks can be great, and I am not against using them. However, I think it can be very problematic if one textbook alone should be the defining voice and the defining source about all matters in a specific subject (Wade & Moje, 2000; Wineburg, 2018). Not only will one textbook always be partial, but also one textbook cannot, regardless of quality, incorporate the local context of each classroom or the context of what is happening in the world that particular day. What texts and what voices to bring into the classroom should be key questions for all teachers. The internet provides endless possibilities here, as many of the tips in this book also show.

Concluding remarks

An important point throughout this book is that using as many digital tools as possible should never be a goal in itself. The goal should rather be to create teaching situations that are engaging and that allows us to help students acquire and show their own knowledge and reflections during their learning process. Digital tools can play a key role in making learning happen – and when that is the case, it has everything to do with the teachers' framing of the learning process and rather little to do with the technology itself.

References

Anderson, S. E., & Maninger, R. M. (2007). Preservice teachers' abilities, beliefs, and intentions regarding technology integration. *Journal of Educational Computing Research*, 37(2), 151–172.

Baker, J. P., Goodboy, A. K., Bowman, N. D., & Wright, A. A. (2018). Does teaching with PowerPoint increase students' learning? A meta-analysis. *Computers & Education*, 126, 376–387.

Baş, G., Kubiatko, M., & Sünbül, A. M. (2016). Teachers' perceptions towards ICTs in teaching-learning process: Scale validity and reliability study. *Computers in Human Behavior*, 61, 176–185.

Baydas, O., & Goktas, Y. (2016). Influential factors on preservice teachers' intentions to use ICT in future lessons. *Computers in Human Behavior*, 56, 170–178.

Bingimlas, K. A. (2009). Barriers to the successful integration of ICT in teaching and learning environments: A review of the literature. *Eurasia Journal of Mathematics, Science & Technology Education*, 5(3), 235–245.

Black, P., Harrison, C., Lee, C., Marshall, B., & Wiliam, D. (2004). Working inside the black box: Assessment for learning in the classroom. *Phi delta kappan*, 86(1), 8–21.

Black, P., & Wiliam, D. (1998). *Inside the black box: Raising standards through classroom assessment*. London: School of Education, King's College.

Black, P., & Wiliam, D. (2009). Developing the theory of formative assessment. *Educational Assessment, Evaluation and Accountability (formerly Journal of Personnel Evaluation in Education)*, 21(1), 5–31.

Blikstad-Balas, M. (2012). Digital literacy in upper secondary school–What do students use their laptops for during teacher instruction? *Nordic Journal of Digital Literacy*, 7(2), 81–96.

Blikstad-Balas, M., & Davies, C. (2017). Assessing the educational value of one-to-one devices: Have we been asking the right questions? *Oxford Review of Education*, 43(3), 311–331.

Blikstad-Balas, M., & Klette, K. (2020). Still a long way to go – Narrow and transmissive use of technology in the classroom. *Nordic Journal of Digital Literacy*, 15(1), 55–68.

Brevik, L. M. (2016). The gaming outliers: Does out-of-school gaming improve boys' reading skills in English as a second language? In E. Elstad (Ed.), *Digital expectations and experiences in education* (pp. 39–61). Rotterdam, the Netherlands: Sense Publishers.

Claro, M., Preiss, D. D., San Martín, E., Jara, I., Hinostroza, J. E., Valenzuela, S., ... Nussbaum, M. (2012). Assessment of 21st century ICT skills in Chile: Test design and results from high school level students. *Computers & Education*, 59(3), 1042–1053.

Delgado, P., Vargas, C., Ackerman, R., & Salmerón, L. (2018). Don't throw away your printed books: A meta-analysis on the effects of reading media on reading comprehension. *Educational Research Review*, 25, 23–38.

Díaz, L. M. B., Garcia, S., & Cano, E. V. (2019). Effects on academic performance in secondary students according to the use of ICT. *IJERI: International Journal of Educational Research and Innovation*, 201812), 90–108.

Dolonen, J. A., & Kluge, A. (2015). *Algebra learning through digital gaming in school. International Society of the Learning Sciences, Inc. [ISLS Conference Proceedings]*. Retrieved from: https://www.isls.org/cscl2015/papers/MC-0232-FullPaper-Dolonen.pdf

Drent, M., & Meelissen, M. (2008). Which factors obstruct or stimulate teacher educators to use ICT innovatively? *Computers & Education*, 51(1), 187–199.

Dunn, J., Gray, C., Moffett, P., & Mitchell, D. (2018). "It's more funner than doing work": Children's perspectives on using tablet computers in the early years of school. *Early Child Development and Care*, 188(6), 819–831.

Elstad, E. (2006). Understanding the nature of accountability failure in a technology-filled, laissez-faire classroom: Disaffected students and teachers who give in. *Journal of Curriculum Studies*, 38(4), 459–481.

Elstad, E. (2016). Educational technology: Expectations and experiences. In E. Elstad (Ed.), *Digital expectations and experiences in education* (pp. 3–28). Rotterdam, the Netherlands: Springer.

Erstad, O. (2006). A new direction? Digital literacy, student participation and curriculum reform in Norway. *Education and Information Technologies*, 11(3–4), 415–429.

Ferrari, A. (2013). *DIGCOMP: A framework for developing and understanding digital competence in Europe*. Luxembourg: Publications Office of the European Union.

Flewitt, R., Messer, D., & Kucirkova, N. (2015). New directions for early literacy in a digital age: The iPad. *Journal of Early Childhood Literacy*, 15(3), 289–310.

Foldvik, M. C. (2015). *Ja, det høres jo riktig ut»-Elevers vurdering av tekster på nett* [Yes, that sound about right: Students' assessment of online texts]. (Master's thesis). University of Oslo.

Gee, J. P., & Hayes, E. R. (2011). *Language and learning in the digital age*. New Yor, NY: Routledge.

Gil-Flores, J., Rodríguez-Santero, J., & Torres-Gordillo, J.-J. (2017). Factors that explain the use of ICT in secondary-education classrooms: The role of teacher characteristics and school infrastructure. *Computers in Human Behavior*, 68, 441–449.

Griffin, P., Care, E., & McGaw, B. (2012). The changing role of education and schools. In P. Griffin, B. McGaw, & E. Care (Eds.), *Assessment and teaching of 21st century skills* (pp. 1–15). Dordrecht, the Netherlands: Springer.

Grimalt-Álvaro, C., Ametller, J., & Pintó, R. (2019). Factors shaping the uptake of ICT in science classrooms. A study of a large-scale introduction of interactive whiteboards and computers. *International Journal of Innovation in Science and Mathematics Education*, 27(1), 18–36

Gudmundsdottir, G. B., & Hatlevik, O. E. (2018). Newly qualified teachers' professional digital competence: implications for teacher education. *European Journal of Teacher Education*, 41(2), 214–231.

Haugerud, T. (2011). Student teachers learning to teach: The mastery and appropriation of digital technology. *Nordic Journal of Digital Literacy*, 6(4), 226–238.

Hennessy, S., & London, L. (2013). *Learning from international experiences with interactive whiteboards: The role of professional development in integrating the technology* (OECD Education Working Papers). Paris, France: OECD.

Howard, S. K., Yang, J., Ma, J., Maton, K., & Rennie, E. (2018). App clusters: Exploring patterns of multiple app use in primary learning contexts. *Computers & Education*, 127, 154–164.

Instefjord, E., & Munthe, E. (2016). Preparing pre-service teachers to integrate technology: An analysis of the emphasis on digital competence in teacher education curricula. *European Journal of Teacher Education*, 39(1), 77–93.

Instefjord, E. J., & Munthe, E. (2017). Educating digitally competent teachers: A study of integration of professional digital competence in teacher education. *Teaching and Teacher Education*, 67, 37–45.

Jewitt, C., Moss, G., & Cardini, A. (2007). Pace, interactivity and multimodality in teachers' design of texts for interactive whiteboards in the secondary school classroom. *Learning, Media and Technology*, 32(3), 303–317.

Klette, K., Sahlström, F., Blikstad-Balas, M., Luoto, J., Tanner, M., Tengberg, M., ... Slotte, A. (2018). Justice through participation: Student engagement in Nordic classrooms. *Education Inquiry*, 9(1), 57–77.

Kucirkova, N., & Sakr, M. (2015). Child–father creative text-making at home with crayons, iPad collage & PC. *Thinking Skills and Creativity*, 17, 59–73.

Lawrence, J. E., & Tar, U. A. (2018). Factors that influence teachers' adoption and integration of ICT in teaching/learning process. *Educational Media International*, 55(1), 79–105.

Lei, J., & Zhao, Y. (2007). Technology uses and student achievement: A longitudinal study. *Computers & Education*, 49(2), 284–296.

Lipowsky, F., Rakoczy, K., Pauli, C., Drollinger-Vetter, B., Klieme, E., & Reusser, K. (2009). Quality of geometry instruction and its short-term impact on students' understanding of the Pythagorean Theorem. *Learning and Instruction*, 19(6), 527–537.

Luke, A. (2019). Regrounding critical literacy: Representation, facts and reality. In D. E. Alvermann, N. J. Unrau, M. Sailors, & R. B. Rudell (Eds.), *Theoretical models and processes of literacy* (7th ed., pp. 349–361). New York, NY: Routledge.

Michelsen, M. (2015). *Teksthendelser i barns hverdag. En tekstetnografisk og sosialsemiotisk studie av åtte barns literacy og deres meninegsskaping på Internett* [Literacy events in childrens daily life. A text ethnographic and social semiotic study of eight childrens' literacy and meaning making on the internet]. (PhD Thesis). University of Oslo.

O'Brien, D., Beach, R., & Scharber, C. (2007). "Struggling" middle schoolers: Engagement and literate competence in a reading writing intervention class. *Reading Psychology*, 28(1), 51–73.

Organisation for Economic Co-operation and Development (OECD). (2015). *Students, computers and learning* (Report). Paris, France: Author.

Player-Koro, C. (2012). Factors influencing teachers' use of ICT in education. *Education Inquiry*, 3(1), 93–108.

Reich, S. M., Yau, J. C., & Warschauer, M. (2016). Tablet-based eBooks for young children: What does the research say? *Journal of Developmental & Behavioral Pediatrics*, 37(7), 585–591.

Røkenes, F. M., & Krumsvik, R. J. (2016). Prepared to teach ESL with ICT? A study of digital competence in Norwegian teacher education. *Computers & Education*, 97, 1–20.

Sahlström, F., Tanner, M., & Valasmo, V. (2019). Connected youth, connected classrooms. Smartphone use and student and teacher participation during plenary teaching. *Learning, Culture and Social Interaction*, 21, 311–331.

Salomon, G. (2016). It's not just the tool but the educational rationale that counts. In E. Elstad (Ed.), *Educational technology and polycontextual bridging* (pp. 149–161). Rotterdam: Springer.

Sana, F., Weston, T., & Cepeda, N. J. (2013). Laptop multitasking hinders classroom learning for both users and nearby peers. *Computers & Education*, 62(0), 24–31. http://dx.doi.org/10.1016/j.compedu.2012.10.003

Sang, G., Valcke, M., Van Braak, J., & Tondeur, J. (2010).

Selwyn, N. (2016). *Is technology good for education?* Cambridge: Polity Press.

Siew, N. M., Geofrey, J., & Lee, B. N. (2016). Students' algebraic thinking and attitudes towards algebra: The effects of game-based learning using DragonBox 12+ app. *The Electronic Journal of Mathematics & Technology*, 10(2).

Silseth, K. (2012). The multivoicedness of game play: Exploring the unfolding of a student's learning trajectory in a gaming context at school. *International Journal of Computer-Supported Collaborative Learning*, 7(1), 63–84.

Støle, H., Mangen, A., & Schwippert, K. (2020). Assessing children's reading comprehension on paper and screen: A mode-effect study. *Computers & Education*, Advanced online publication. https://www.sciencedirect.com/science/article/pii/S0360131520300610

Tømte, C. E. (2013). Educating teachers for the new millennium?-Teacher training, ICT and digital competence. *Nordic Journal of Digital Literacy* (Special annirversay issue reprint 2015), 138–154.

Valtonen, T., Pontinen, S., Kukkonen, J., Dillon, P., Väisänen, P., & Hacklin, S. (2011). Confronting the technological pedagogical knowledge of Finnish net generation student teachers. *Technology, Pedagogy and Education*, 20(1), 3–18. doi:10.1080/1475939X.2010.534867

Wade, S. E., & Moje, E. B. (2000). The role of text in classroom learning. In M. L. Kamil, P. B. Mosenthal, D. B. Pearson, & R. Barr (Eds.), *Handbook of reading research* (Vol. 3, pp. 609–627). New York, NY: Erlbaum.

Westlund, O., & Bjur, J. (2014). Media life of the young. *Young*, 22(1), 21–41.

Wineburg, S. (2018). *Why learn history (When it's already on your phone)*. Chicago, IL: University of Chicago Press.

Index

Page numbers in *italics* refer to content in *figures*.

academic performance 28; success factors 22
Act2connect.us 48–49
adaptability 5, 6, 18, 67, 83, 86
advanced searches 17, 32, 93
advertising 93
algebra 12–13, 56, 111, 115, 118, 120
anatomy 108
Anderson, J. 2
Anki 65
Anonymity 28, 31, 62, 64
Apple 47, 52, 56, 57, 59, 73
apps 4, 58–59, 113, 114–115; benefits for education 111; mathematics 55–56, *56*
architecture 108, 109
assessment: "formative" versus "summative" 12, 27, 52, 58, 118
Audacity (open-source software) 34
audio 23, 32–33, 57, 58, 66, 101, 108
augmented reality (AR) 108–109
Azam, N. A. 27
Azzam, A. M. 13

background noise 98
BBC 39, 49–50
Bekkestua: Nadderud High School 14
Bergen: Nordahl Grieg Upper Secondary School 78; Rothaugen Middle School 46
Bergmann, Jonathan 69–70, 72, 77
Bing 18, 93, 105
Black Lives Matter 47
Blikstad-Balas, Marte 3, 6, 99, 102, 110–120
block scheduling 4, 9–11; classroom application 10–11; lesson plan 11; success criterion 10; writing for real audience about issues that matter 10–11
blogging: improvement of writing skills 27–28; to publish 40
blogs 8, 11, 20, 31, 32, 39, 43, 44, 48, 111; classroom application 42
bookmarks 19, 21, 97
Boolean Search 17
BP 94
Brevik, L. M. 110
Brexit 17, 39, *89*, *96*
browsers 25, 31, 42, 103

Camtasia Studio 33
Canada 60
Canady, R. L. 10
Care-Mail 46–47
Carr, Nicholas: *Shallows* (2010) 97
chemistry 69, 82
children 84–85
China 18, 44
Cirillo, Francesco 97
Class notebooks 23–24
classroom discussion 32, 71, 74, 77, 79, 80, 82, 85–86, 116
classroom management 58, 67; in some things to consider 11; in student ownership of learning 5; in technology in school 5, 40, 110, 112
climate change 7–8, 14, *22*
cloud storage 24, 25; classroom application 26–27; *see also* Google Drive
ClustrMap 40, *41–42*
CNN 39

Cobarrubia, Frank 47
Coggle 23
cognitive activation 116–117
commognition (Sfard) 57
computers 1, 4, 5, 9, 14, 19, 23, 32, 61, 99, 112, 116 *et passim*
conferences 25, 37, 38, 70, 76
conflicts 39, 46, 53, 72, 111
connectivity 117; knowledge sources and subjects 7; technology, pedagogy, content 4
consent 92
continuing professional development 3, 38, 40, 44, 113, 114, 119
cooperative learning 4, 60–68, 71, 92; apps for learning new material 65; definition 60; find someone who 66, *66*; jigsaw (reading new material) 65; parking lot 62, *63*; presentations 65–66; send a problem 67; think-pair-share 63–64; way of future 67
cooperative learning (basic elements) 60–61; equal participation 60, 61; face-to-face promotive interaction 61; individual and group accountability 61; positive interdependence 60, 61; social skills training 61
copyright rules 90
coronavirus pandemic 34–35, 46; effect on schooling in Norway 49–50; game-changer (2020) 1; impact on teaching and learning 1–3; school closures (worldwide) 2
counterfactual history 82
Creative Commons 32
creativity 6–9, 23, 35, 67, 79, 88, 102, 111, 119; musical 52–53
critical thinking 7, 8, 53, 88, 90, 116; *see also* reflection
Crouch, C. H. 64, 68
cultural artifacts 80–81
curriculum 7, 11, 46, 113, 118; content 81, 82
curriculum goals 11, *12*, 12, 22, 44, 45, 70, 72, 97, 107

D'Anza, J. 34
decision-making 27, 46, 81, 83–84, 86, 90, 94
deeper learning 6–7, 11, 97; classroom application 7–9; competencies required 6; interpretations 7
democracy 89, 94–95, 100
Democracy 3 (role-play and simulation) 83–84
dictation functions 101, 102, *103*, 104
digital citizenship 4, 13, 17, 45, 88–100; class discussions 92–93; classroom applications 91, 95; curriculum vitae for future jobs 91; cyberbullying 88, 90, 92–93; digital footprint 90–91; "has to be taught in context" 100; online etiquette 92; planning time spent online 95–97; purpose 100; searching online 93–95; sharing pictures online 91–93; use of multiple sources to verify information 95
digital classroom: block scheduling 9–11; global classroom with personal learning networks 13–14; new ways of learning 4–15; pedagogy for deeper learning 6–9; student ownership 11–13; technology 5–6
digital classroom (research insights) 5, 102, 110–120; access to hardware and software 112–113; cognitive activation 116–117; connecting to outside world 117; learning process (tracing) 115; positive and negative findings 110–112; recommendations (successful implementation factors) 114–117; teacher technology 114–115; teachers' attitudes and competence 112, 113–114
digital competence 6, 94, 102, 110, 111, 113–114, 118–120
digital devices: benefits for education 111; use in cooperative learning 61–67
digital discernment 90, 93
digital field trips 81–85
digital footprint 90–91
digital pens 64, 73
digital tools 4, 16–36, 64, 65, 72, 93, 97, 99; annotating and writing together 20–27; audio and video recordings 32–33; demonstrating mastery 27–35; learning online 34–35; searching and keeping track of information 16–20; use of "never a goal in itself" 117
Diigo 19
disease 85
Dog Island 95
DragonBox 111, 115
Drent, M. 114, 118
Dropbox 24–27
DuckDuckGo 18
Dweck, Carol 12
dynamic graphs 55
dynamic mathematics software 56
dysgraphia 104, 105
dyslexia 65, 101–105

eBooks 112, 120
Ecosia 19
edublogs 40

EdWordle: classroom application 21; keywords 20; starting thought processes 20
Ellison, K. 47
emotional dilemmas 83
employers 91; job market 67
English as second language 72, 110–111, 118
ethical dilemmas 82, 83
ethics 90–91
ewordle.net 20
examination nerves 58
examinations 21, 23, 24, 34, 55, 56, 71, 72
Expeditions app 107, 108
Explain Everything 57, 69; layout 74; mathematics 73–75; recording entire lessons 73; tips 75; tools 73, 73; videos 72–75
exploratory talk 21

face-to-face promotive interaction 61; time 69
Facebook 5, 14, 39, 44, 48, 88, 91–93; classroom application 46–47; networking 45–47
fake news 95
Fallen of World War II (video) 53
feedback 27, 28–32, 42, 61, 62, 64, 72, 75, 115
Feedly 42, 43, *43*
Ferguson riots (2014) 47
file-sharing 25–27
Fleischer, Elaine 14
Flewitt, R. 111
flipped classroom 4, 32, 33, 57, 69–77; application 71–72; Explain Everything videos 72–75; note-taking from instructional videos 71–72, 77; pedagogical theory 69–71; points before starting 77; practical examples 71–72; valuable parts 77; video-recording 72
Foldnes, N. 71, 77
Fullan, M. 7, 8

Gabrielsen, Lisa 49–50
Gapminder 53–55; questions answered (examples) *54*; search categories *54*
GarageBand app 52, 59
GenoChoice website 95
GeoGebra 56; functions *56*
Gilley, Jeremy 44
"Girls in India" 47
global classroom 4, 13–14; social media 37–50
Global Conflicts: Palestine (game) 111
Gone Home (games as narratives) 83, 84
Goodhart's law 99
Google 1, 16, 37, 46, 53, 89, 91–94, 97, 116; Advanced Search filter "Usage rights" 32; alternative search engines 18–19; Be Internet Awesome website 92; Digital Safety Resources 92; searching particular country or domain 17–18; specific searches 17
Google Chrome 19, 25, 31, 95, 98, 103
Google Docs 25, 64, 67, 99, 102, 103, 112, 115
Google Drive 25, 66; classroom application 26
Google Scholar 18
goSupermodel website 92
grammar 28, 31, 70, 71
Grammarly 31
Grimalt-Álvaro, C. 114, 119
guitar 51–53, 58

Handeland, Tobias Langås 48–49
hardware 79, 112–113
hashtags 38
headphones 108
Hennessy, S. 111, 119
high schools 10, 64, 108; warnings to students about digital traps 93
history as a subject taught 46, 53, 72, 82, 84–85, 117
homeschooling 1, 2
homework 70, 96
Hootsuite 38
Hopfenbeck, T. N. 28
Husøy, Aleksander 78–87

images (reusable) 31
Immersive Reader 65
iMovie 57
India 8, 47
information competence 90
innovation 7–9, 56, 67, 108, 118
Instagram 5, 45, 91–93
interaction 9, 20, 37, 52, 61, 62, 67, 111
interactivity 72, 77, 86, 111, 119
interference in elections *89–90*
International Computer and Information Literacy Study (ICILS) 94
International Society for Technology in Education 70
internet 42, 88, 90, 97, 111, 117
internet access 5, 32
interviews 10, 34, 58, 66
IOS iPad 72
iPads 4, 65; music lessons 51–53; Numbers app 56
iPhone 52, 56
iPod 56
Israel 8, 111
"Its learning" 12, 29–31

Johannesburg 31
Johnson, D.W. 60, 62, 68
Johnson, R.T. 60, 62, 68
Journal of Consumer Research 98
journalism and what to trust 95

Kahoot! 32, 65, 91, 99, 112, 116
Khan Academy 69, 75, *76*
Kindle 47, 65
knowledge 6–8, 22, 32, 34, 45, 48, 53, 67, 72, 78–80, 88, 94, 102, 106, 111, 115–117
Krumsvik, R. J. 113, 120
Kucirkova, N. 111

laboratory work 107, 108
language learning 44, 102, *103*; flipped classroom 70, 71; video games 83
Langworthy, M. 7, 8
laptop computers 79, 111, 113, 118, 120; note-taking 64, 68
Lassiter, Chad Dion 47
learning disabilities 101
learning goals 64, 115; versus performance goals 12–13
learning online 34–35, *41*, 47, 48, 75, 90 *et passim*
learning partners 63, 74–75
learning platform 12, 21, 58
learning process 115, 117; assessment 57–58
learning structures 62
lecturing 5, 8, 10, 64–65, 68, 71, 76
Lesotho: Mamoeketsi Primary School 48–49
Lifewire 33
Liner 19–20
Lipowsky, F. 116, 119
literacy software 101–105
literature 80–81, 84
London, L. 111, 119
London School of Business 34
Lynch, M. 6

Mac computer 4, 33, 72
MacOS 34, 98
Mankato (Minnesota) 95
Marr, B. 109
Massachusetts 14
Massachusetts Institute of Technology 8
mathematics 85, 111, 115; apps and video 51, 55–57; Explain Everything videos 73–75; flipped classroom 70–72
McGrane, J. A. 28
medical students 108

Meelissen, M. 114, 118
memory cards 65
Michaelsen, Ann S. 42, 115; *Connected Learners* (2013) 13, 42; "Connected Teaching and Learning" blog (2008–) 40, *40–41*; English teacher 4, 10; hits *41*; school leader 4, 10, 61; visitor map *41*; webpage 27
Michaelsen, Sigurd A. 72–73
Microsoft cloud 24; *see also* OneDrive
Microsoft Office 365, 23, 25, 26, 33, 66, 67
Microsoft PowerPoint 23, 99, 112, 113, 116; presentations 5, 25, 35, 64, 65; Slide Show feature 33
Microsoft Teams 1, 35, 49, 64
Microsoft Word: dictation facility 102, *103*; Researcher 105, *106*; Smart Lookup 105, *106–107*; thesaurus feature 103; Track Changes function 115; Translate 105, *106*
middle schools 4, 46, 64, 94; use of tablet PCs 51–59, 69
mind maps 22–23; apps 23
MindMup 23
Mitchell, David 29
mixed reality 108–109
mobile telephones 5, 33, 34, 72, 85, 91, 97, 99
Moodle 70
moral philosophy 83
Movie Maker 66
Multi-Touch gestures 56, 57
multimedia 55
multimodality 55, 57, 119
multiple choice 8, 32
multisensory processing 104
music: improvisation stage 53; interaction and rhythm 52; soundtrack 66
music lessons: apps 51–53; classroom application 53; video logs 58
My Child: Lebensborn (games as digital field trips) 83–85
Mystery Skype 45

narrative podcasts 34
networking 38, 44, 48; Facebook 45–47
networks 5, 13–14, 16, 19, 27, 31, 43, 77
New Orleans 46
New York Times: "Daily" podcast 33–34
Newsguard 89, 95
Nisted, Inger-Merethe 72
Norway 1, 23, 24, 26, 33, 34, 40, 45, 47, 50, 53, 58, 67, 71, 72, 92, 97, 101, 108; climate change 8; Department of Education 7; digital infrastructure (utilization) 112–113;

high schools 10; international collaboration 48–49; new curricula (2020) 6
Nouri, J. 70
November, Alan 94
nude pictures 92

O'Brien, D. 111, 119
Oculus Rift headsets 108
OneDrive 23, 26–27
OneNote 23, 31, 65, 67, 97; audio and video facilities 24; classroom application 24
OneNote Class notebook 12, 24, 27, 64, 66, 70
OneNote Learning Tools: Immersive Reader *104*, 104; Picture Dictionary 104, *105*
online behaviour 90–91
online nicknames 92
online safety 90–93, 100
Opava City (CR): Mendel Grammar School 108
Organisation for Economic Co-operation and Development (OECD) 2, 67, 88, 94; PISA tests 111
Oslo: Sandvika High School (2006–) 4, 48–50, 72

Padlet 8, 46, 50, 62, *63*, 89, 115, 116; classroom application 21, *22*; idea development and notes 21
Pandolpho, B. 10
Pariser, Eli: "filter bubble" 94
parking lot 62, *63*
Peace One Day 44
pedagogy 4, 35, 37, 39, 45, 59, 99, 114, 120; deeper learning 6–8, 14; digital 13; flipped classroom 69–71; tablet PCs 51, 59; traditional 1; transmissive 116; video games 78–87
Pedersen, Terje 46–47
peer assessment 27, 28–32, 35, 115
peer instruction (PI) 64
PEGI age ratings 83
personal computers 4, 72, 85, 91, 97, 108
personal learning networks 13–14, 16, 31
physics 82–83
piano 52–53
Picard, Rosalind 8
Pingo app 64
Pink, Daniel 12–13
plagiarism 55, 102
Plague Inc. (games as simulations) 83, 85
Player-Koro, C. 114, 120
podcasts 33–34, 69

Pomodoro apps 98
Pomodoro Technique 71, 97–99; classroom application 99
population growth 53, *54*
poverty 53, *54*
presentations 5, 23–25, 32, 33, 35, 55, 58, 64–66, 101
Price, G. A. 102
primary schools 4, 48–49, 58, 92
prison systems 46
privacy threats 88
problem-solving 6, 7, 67, 69–70, 74, 77, 90, 115
proofreading 39

quadblogging.com 29–31
QuickTime Player 33
Quizlet 65
quizzes 8, 32, 65

Read Aloud function 102–104, *103*
reading comprehension 111
reading proficiency 110–111
Reagan, Ronald 95
real world 6, 80, 82, 109
reality gap: value as learning experience 82
Really Simple Syndication (RSS) 27, 42; classroom application 43, *43*
reflection 6–8, 21, 22, 53, 55, 61, 63, 64, 77, 86, 90, 93, 116, 117; *see also* thinking
Reich, S. M. 112, 120
religion 37, 44, 72
Rettig, M. D. 10
reward and punishment 13
Rheingold, Howard 94
rhinoceroses 44–45
risk management 88
Røkenes, F. M. 113, 120
role play 78, 81–83, 84

Safari 95
safe classroom environment 61, 62, 67
Sakr, M. 111
Sams, Aaron 69–70, 72, 77
Schleicher, Andreas 2, 3
science 72, 111
Screencast-O-Matic 33
screenshots 23, 58, 74, 91
searching online 16–20, 93–95, 105, *106–107*
Sekese, Moliehi 48
Sfard, A. 57
Siew, N. M. 111, 120
Silseth, K. 111, 120

SimpleMind 23
simulation 81, 83–84, 85, 87
skimming 97
Skype 8, 14, 38, 46, 48, 71; classroom application 44–45; uses 44
smart lenses 109
smartboards 99, 112
smartphones 32, 108, 109, 111
Snapchat 5, 13, 45, 91, 92
social bookmarking 19
social media 1, 5, 14, 21, 71, 77, 90–92, 94, 100, 111, 113; global classroom 4, 27, 37–50; international collaboration between schools 48–49; reaching out to wider audience 49–50; usefulness 37
social science lessons 53, *54*; classroom application 55; group interviews 58; online resources 53–55; video games 83, 85
software 1, 23–26, 31–35, 43, 58–59
software access 112–113
sources (reliability) 13, 16, 31, 47, 55, 88, 93, 94–95, 116
South Africa 44
South Dakota 46
special needs education 65, 101–109; apps and games 108; literacy software 101–105; searching for information 105, *106–107*; VR glasses in class 105–109
spell-checker 31, 102, 103
spreadsheets 55–56
Spurkland, Simen 51–59, 115
Staaby, Tobias 78–87
Stanne, M. 62, 68
Startpage 18
Statista 2
statistics 53, 56
story-telling 34
student-centered learning 5, 10, 12, 59
students: adaptability 6, 18, 67; agency 12, 81; cognitive activation 116–117; comprehension 22, 46, 64, 97, 104, 111, 118, 120; cyberbullying 88, 90, 92–93; demonstrating mastery 27–35, 57–71 *passim*, 97, 104; digital traps for the unwary 92–93; effort 13, 22, 49, 61, 116; empowerment 7, 10, 75, 88, 90; empowerment through blogging 27–28; engagement 8, 11–13, 22, 46, 64, 66, 70, 88, 95, 106, 116, 119; explorative 6, 21, 88; intelligence 22, 101; motivation 11–13, 22, 27, 29, 31, 32, 42, 46, 57, 70, 107, 117; one device each 4, 5, 9, 112–114, 116; ownership of learning 11–13; role of researcher 9; self-control 5, 98; self-discipline 99; self-efficacy 29; Six Cs of Education 7; twenty-first century skills 7, 119; voice and choice 3, 55, 59
Super Mario 79
surgeons 108–109
surveys 32, 45

tablet computers 19, 23, 25, 32, 85, 91, 99, 109–112, 114, 116, 120; use in middle schools 4, 51–59
tag clouds 64
tagging 23, 39
Talkwall 62, 115; classroom application 21; participants at different locations 21
teacher awareness 104
teacher quality 59
teachers: digital competence 2–3, 6, 102; framing of learning process 117; role models 93
technology 4, 5–6, 70, 100, 101, 114–115 *et passim*
TED Talks 40, 69, 76
TED-Ed: flipped classroom 76–77
teenagers 14, 48–50
terabyte 26
tests 6, 8, 12, 21, 23, 32, 57, 58, 66, 71, 72, 75, 99, 106, 111
text (reusable) 32
textbooks 1, 8, 13, 58, 64, 74, 106, 117
text-highlighting 19; Liner (classroom application) 19–20
thinking 8, 57, 60, 67, 80, 88, 111, 115, 116, 120; *see also* critical thinking
think-pair-share notes 64–65
Thunberg, G. 8
time spent in school 9–10, 69–70, 72, 115; spent online 95–97
time zones problem 44
trust 92–94
"trust but verify" (Russian proverb) 95
TweetDeck 38
Twitter 14, 44, 45, 47; advice for users 39; classroom application 38–39; #edchat 38; source of information 37–42; tweets and retweets 38
Twitter dictionary 39–40

UNESCO 1
United Kingdom 17; England 31; Northern Ireland 46

United States 10, 31, 38, 44, 46, 47; presidential election (2020) *90*
University of Oslo 5, 21
UN Sustainable Development Goals 7–8
usernames and passwords 92

video games: advice 86; benefits for education 111; in classroom 79, 83–85; cultural artifacts 80–81; definition of "affordance" 78–79; digital field trips 81–85; educational affordances 78–81; framing by teacher in curricular context 82; guidelines from teachers (focus on lesson objectives) 86; important considerations 85–86; pre- and post-activities 80; relationship between virtual and real 79–80; role-play 81–84; teacher-flexibility 86; variable quality 80–81
video games (examples): Democracy 3 (role-play and simulation) 83–84; Gone Home (games as narratives) 83, 84; My Child: Lebensborn (games as digital field trips) 83–85; Plague Inc. (games as simulations) 83, 85
video games pedagogy 4, 78–87
video logs 52, 55, 57–58
videos 13, 21, 23, 32–34, 39, 40, 49, 101, 106; classroom application 33; instructional 35, 69–70, 75; mathematics 56–57; music lessons 53; reusable 32
Vietnam War 46

virtual reality technology 101; VR glasses 105–109
vision 48, 61, 114
vocational training courses 85
Vygotskian model 102

Washington Post 46–47, 50
websites 90, 92, 95, 97, 105; blocking apps 98
Weingartner, N. P. 9
West Coast (USA) 84
whiteboard 64, 71, 72, 74, 111, 119
Wikimedia Commons 32
Wikipedia 105
Windows 34, 102
Wineburg, Sam: *Why Learn History?* (2018) 117
Wolfram Alpha 19
Word 23, 27, 31
word clouds 20–21
Word Online 64
WordPress 40; "Visibility Public" option 42
World War I 47
World War II 55, 84, 116
writing together 20–27

Yahoo! 93
Yandex 19
Yippy Search 19
YouTube 13, 21, 53, 69, 72, 75

Zoom 1, 34–35, 46

For Product Safety Concerns and Information please contact our EU representative GPSR@taylorandfrancis.com
Taylor & Francis Verlag GmbH, Kaufingerstraße 24, 80331 München, Germany

www.ingramcontent.com/pod-product-compliance
Lightning Source LLC
Chambersburg PA
CBHW082101230426
43670CB00017B/2918